Teacher Thinking
and the Case Method

Theory and Future Directions

Teacher Thinking
and the Case Method

Theory and Future Directions

Amy Raths McAninch

*with a Foreword
by Robert Floden*

TEACHERS
COLLEGE
PRESS

Teachers College
Columbia University
New York and London

Published by Teachers College Press, 1234 Amsterdam Avenue
New York, New York 10027

Library of Congress Cataloging-in-Publication Data

McAninch, Amy Raths.
    Teacher thinking and the case method : theory and future
    directions / Amy Raths McAninch.
        p.   cm.
    Includes bibliographical references (p.   ) and index.
    ISBN 0-8077-3243-5 (alk. paper)
    1. Teachers—Training of.   2. Case method.   I. Title.
LB1707.M32   1993
370.71—dc20   93-18207

ISBN 0-8077-3243-5

Printed on acid-free paper

Manufactured in the United States of America

99 98 97 96 95 94 93   8 7 6 5 4 3 2 1

**For my parents,
James D. Raths and Leslie van Riper Raths.**

Contents

Foreword

Much has been written recently about the role that case studies can or should play in teacher education. This surge of interest stems in part from changes in social science. Recognizing that teaching and learning are complex processes, investigators have shifted from seeking simple laws of learning to providing thick descriptions of educational episodes. A glance at the educational journals and books from the past decade shows a marked increase in the space devoted to lesson transcripts, detailed records of observations, and vivid descriptions of teachers and students. In some measure, therefore, the increased use of case studies in teacher education follows the increased importance of cases in educational research.

Reliance on the case method also reflects an aspiration to follow the path taken by more prestigious and remunerative professions, such as medicine, law, and business. Teacher educators hope that adapting preparation methods from these professions will enhance the status of their own occupation. To plan for use of the case method, teacher educators have begun to consider what changes are needed to fit the particular context of their profession. Discussions of case methods in teacher education often consider whether the difference in underlying disciplines (e.g., psychology rather than biology) should lead to changes in approach or whether the absence of precedents and of a systematic case literature poses an obstacle.

Missing from discussions about the case method in teacher education has been attention to teachers as learners. Who are the students of teacher education? What is known about how those students learn? What things are teachers likely to learn while at the university or while on the job? What learning is most important at each point in a teacher's career? How might answers to these questions affect the case method's applicability?

Amy McAninch's book fills this gap with thoughtful analyses that draw on scholarship from several disciplines. She argues that decisions about teacher preparation must be grounded in an understanding of how teachers learn, of what they see as the sources of teaching knowledge, and of how their workplaces influence what and how they will continue to learn. An understanding of teachers' cognitive development is required to appreciate the likely effects of formal teacher education. A close look at teachers' classrooms is necessary to ground judgments about the aims of teacher preparation. Arguments for adapting case study methods to teacher preparation must be based in close attention to the special character of teachers and classrooms.

In the first chapter, the argument begins with a concise summary of the literature highlighting the practical orientation of teachers' thinking. As McAninch points out, this "clinical consciousness" is a product both of classroom demands and of the ideology prevalent in U.S. education. The action orientation and its roots are important parts of the context for planning teacher education programs. If attempts to strengthen the theoretical bases of teaching practice are to have any hope of success, they must take account of the prevalence and functionality of clinical consciousness.

In this century, most public school teachers have been women. Other scholars have considered this fact's significance for the structure and status of the occupation and for teaching's place in women's lives. In the second chapter, McAninch makes an important contribution by showing how the "feminization" of teaching sets teacher education apart from other professional studies. Because of the large proportion of women entering teaching, teachers are more likely than doctors, lawyers, or business executives to begin their preparation with views inclined toward clinical consciousness. Beliefs about sources of knowledge are critical for what teachers study and learn at the university and on the job. McAninch reminds us that typical teacher education practices may reinforce the view that knowledge in teaching is either subjective or prescriptive.

Chapter 3 returns attention to clinical consciousness. McAninch shows that clinical consciousness inhibits improvement, even though it is a functional response to the immediate demands of practice. Rather than learning from their mistakes, teachers repeat them. Rather than turning to experts for ways of understanding their situation, teachers either look for packaged solutions or simply go it alone. In any case, they do not ordinarily adopt the scientific stance—so well articulated by John Dewey—that undergirds reflection. If case studies—or any other innovations in teacher preparation—are to support reflective practice, they must help teachers see the value of systematic investigations and theory.

In Chapter 4, McAninch shows why the case study approaches dominant in other professions are not well suited to teacher education. Although each approach attempts to help practitioners see connections between theory and practice, none seems likely to promote the shift in thinking needed for typical teacher education students. For teacher education, the approach must link theory and practice, but must do so in a way that will promote connected understanding.

Chapter 5 lays out a case study approach that does fit with the goals and students of teacher education. Using ideas from Joseph Schwab's seminal papers on "the practical," McAninch outlines what cases should be like and how they should be used. By grounding this proposal in the previous analyses, she argues that her approach has a better chance of helping teachers develop a connected view of knowing that draws on their own strengths and provides a basis for collective, systematic learning. The final chapter provides some concrete examples—cases of case teaching—to allow the reader to connect theory and practice in teacher education.

Clear expositions of clinical consciousness, the demands of teaching, the limits of learning from experience, and the varieties of case method would, on their own, make this a valuable text. Each of these areas are important in understanding teacher education. The book's strong original contribution, however, lies in grounding a proposal for teacher education in an analysis of how teachers think, especially how they think about their own learning. Scholars now advocate greater attention to student conceptions of subject matter. McAninch takes this advice to heart in her study of teacher education itself. In so doing, she shows how case study approaches can address a perennial problem: helping teachers connect theory and practice in ways that help them to continue learning.

Robert E. Floden
Michigan State University

Preface

In 1986, when I began developing preliminary ideas for this manuscript, little research on case methods in teacher education had been published. That spring, Lee Shulman's important essay on the knowledge base of teaching was published in *Educational Researcher*. There he suggested that the case method may have an important role to play in the education of teachers. That essay spurred many subsequent inquiries on case methods, including this one. In the summer of 1986, I had the opportunity to work with Harry Broudy, Steve Tozer, and William Trent at the University of Illinois as they attempted to develop a case method project stemming from Broudy's ideas about the need in teacher education for a "consensus of the learned." The idea that Broudy advanced—that the construction of cases as "standard problems" might help stabilize the field—was intriguing to me. The opportunity to work on this project pushed me to think further about teacher education in general. These events, combined with a course in which I enrolled on research in teacher education, taught by James Raths and Lilian Katz, motivated me to pursue this work.

Although this book is about the case method and proposes a case method for teacher education drawn from the work of Schwab (1978a, 1978b), it is also about the consciousness of teachers and the reasons, based on this theoretical understanding, for the use of the case method in the classroom. These ideas, which are presented in Chapters 1–3, are, I feel, the most important in this work. In Chapter 1, I use Freidson's (1970) concept of clinical mentality to describe the consciousness of teachers generally. I argue that the organizational conditions of work for most teachers facilitate the development of a consciousness that is oppressive and socially reproductive. At the conclusion of that chapter, I link "clinical consciousness" to broader ideological forces in society and try to show that this perspective is endemic to our culture as a whole. These political implications of clinical consciousness are worthy of further research.

In Chapter 2, I explore levels of consciousness that were posited by Belenky and her co-authors (1986) in their work, *Women's Ways of Knowing*, and suggest that clinical consciousness may be a developmental phenomenon, and, if so, that there may be pedagogical interventions that might be useful in spurring the growth of teachers toward other orientations.

The works of Dewey are used in Chapter 3 to critique clinical consciousness as a perspective. There I argue that clinical consciousness leads to inferential error, impedes learning from sources other than firsthand experience, and blocks critical inquiry into schooling. Dewey (1904) argued for a different consciousness for teachers, and in Chapter 3 I link his ideas about the orientation toward knowing that teachers should have with the work of Belenky et al. (1986). In that chapter, I preliminarily suggest that case methods might be useful as a pedagogy for promoting epistemological growth.

The remaining three chapters of this work focus on case methods. In Chapter 4, I reviewed the case methods in law, medicine, and business and offered reasons why they are inappropriate models for teacher education. Teacher educators have most frequently cited the business case method as a precedent for our field; yet, there may be more appropriate models in fields that have historically educated women, such as social work and nursing.

In Chapter 5, an outline of a case method is offered that I think contributes to teachers' theoretical understanding, epistemological growth, and the disposition to bring principles to cases. These goals are seen as a means of developing the kind of perspective Dewey (1904) advocated teachers hold in their practice. Finally, the last chapter offers case materials for this case method. It is my hope that teacher educators will find this work helpful in their quest to improve the practice of teacher education.

Acknowledgments

Over the five years during which this text evolved from a dissertation to its current form, many individuals have given me their support, encouragement, and insights. First, I would like to thank my original doctoral committee, Ralph Page, Lilian Katz, and James Anderson (all of the University of Illinois), and Philip L. Smith of Ohio State University. Ralph Page directed my thesis research with his characteristic patience, generosity, and care. I also benefitted from working on the Illinois Case Method Project, directed by Harry Broudy, Steve Tozer, and William Trent. I also am grateful for the opportunity to have worked with the late Susan Rosenholtz, who contributed greatly to my understanding of school culture and norms.

I would also like to acknowledge the support for this work that I received at Knox College in Galesburg, Illinois, from my colleague Lanny Beyer; from our departmental secretary, Peggy Danielson; and from a group of remarkable students who, over a span of two years, provided some very valuable research assistance. They include: Joni Garlock, Keith vander Meulen, William Feste, Chris Sturm, and especially Mariah Oxford, who not only performed the usual menial tasks associated with research assistance, but whose critical feedback was extremely helpful. I also want to thank the dean of the college, John Strassburger, for supporting this work with research funds. Finally, I appreciate the students who enrolled in the courses I taught at Knox and who helped me gain a better understanding of the theory and practice of teacher education.

My family has also played an ongoing role in supporting this work, and I am very indebted to them. Since I come from a family of teacher educators, their contribution has been affective and intellectual. My husband, Stuart McAninch, of the University of Missouri—Kansas City, has pushed me to understand the ideological implications of clinical consciousness, and I am grateful to him for that. This work would not have been started or completed without the guidance and direction provided by my father, James

Raths, of the University of Delaware. My mother, Leslie Raths, provided editorial suggestions on every draft and patiently reread
each version. Both of my parents instilled in me a commitment to
making the quality of teaching and learning in the public schools
better.

Finally, I would like to thank several individuals at Teachers
College Press: Sarah Biondello, Susan Liddicoat, and Neil
Stillman. I am grateful to all of them for their patience, generosity,
and skill in guiding this work through the editorial and produc-
tion process. I would also like to express my gratitude to Bob Floden for contributing the foreword to this volume.

Teacher Thinking
and the **Case Method**

Theory and Future Directions

1

Clinical Consciousness and the Practice of Teaching

> These recruits who face teaching as a life work are ready to learn
> to teach, and they are ready, though they know it not, to be
> formed by teaching. When teaching has formed them, what
> shape will it give them? Their daily work will write upon them;
> what will it write?
> —Willard Waller, *The Sociology of Teaching*, 1967; p. 380

Teaching no doubt writes many things on its practitioners. Waller
(1932) argued that over time this particular occupational role "ties
to the inner frame of personality" such character traits as inflexi-
bility and reserve (p. 381). A study from outside the field of teacher
education suggests a different partial answer to Waller's question:
namely, that teaching promotes and sustains a particular orientation toward knowing, problem solving, and acting. In describing
teachers' perspectives, it is useful to turn to Freidson's (1970) study
of the medical profession. In *Profession of Medicine*, he argued that
the "everyday physician" is repeatedly called upon to solve concrete, often complex problems, largely in isolation from his or her
colleagues. This setting and the demands of practice, Freidson
wrote, give rise to a worldview quite different from the orientation
of medical researchers or physicians who work in research settings. This worldview he called the "clinical mentality." In the following pages, Freidson's construct will be applied to the field of
teaching; however, the term *clinical consciousness* will be used to
denote the perspective he described because the term *mentality*
tends to carry negative connotations. To the extent that teachers
can be characterized by this worldview, a point that will be discussed at length below, their ability to productively learn from
their own experience, as well as from the experience of researchers, is compromised. In other words, teachers' orientation toward
knowing, their clinical consciousness, may in part provide an ex-

1

planation for the persistent gap between theory and practice in education.

Examination of Freidson's (1970) work is warranted for several reasons. First, although Freidson's study examined the medical profession in particular, and his description of clinical mentality is based on his study of physicians, his analysis extends beyond medicine. Looking at medicine as an exemplar of a profession, Freidson studied the structure of the occupation, medical education, and medical research to understand more clearly the nature of these phenomena in the professions generally. Thus, Freidson's work cannot be taken as an inquiry into the medical profession exclusively, but rather as a work with broad implications for other fields as well.

Second, while medical clinical work and teaching are obviously disparate practices in many ways, these fields share several elements. For example, teachers, like everyday physicians, are pressed to respond to concrete problems for which there may or may not be a standard response, generally in isolation from their colleagues. If this type of experience induces a clinical worldview, as Freidson asserted, then his construct may well apply to the educational domain. In this chapter, Freidson's construct "clinical mentality" will be introduced, and it will be argued that it aptly describes the worldview of teachers generally.

THE CLINICAL MIND

Freidson (1970) found that clinicians' "way of looking at the world" (p. 169) is characterized by five elements:

1. An orientation to action
2. A faith in the efficacy of one's actions
3. A reliance on firsthand experience in decision making
4. A crudely pragmatic approach to solving problems
5. A distrust for generalization

These five elements are described more fully below.

First, the clinically minded are oriented to action and tend to feel compelled to intervene when faced with a problem or a demanding client. According to Freidson, the compulsion to take action persists even when the rationale for intervention is unclear:

> Successful action is preferred, but action with very little chance
> for success is to be preferred over no action at all. There is a
> tendency for the practitioner to take action for its own sake on
> the spurious assumption that doing something is better than do-
> ing nothing. (p. 168)

In attempting to solve concrete problems, the clinically minded
are unlikely to favor running tests, studying the problem further,
or reading an instructor's manual. They are more likely to attempt
an intervention.

Second, individuals who are clinically minded tend to have
faith that their efforts make a difference. This confidence in the
efficacy of one's work allows the clinician to keep taking actions
for which there may or may not be a scientific rationale:

> Given a commitment to action and practical solution, in the face
> of ambiguity the practitioner is more likely to manifest a certain
> will to believe in the value of his actions than to manifest a
> skeptical detachment. . . . How could a present-day psychiatrist
> work if he really believed the careful studies which emphasize
> the unreliability of diagnosis and the undemonstrability of suc-
> cess of psychotherapy? (pp. 168–169)

The doctor, Freidson asserted, is a "placebo reactor" (p. 168),
whose confidence translates into changes in the medical care provided and wins the compliance of patients who consequently
agree to follow the doctor's orders.

Third, a "crude" pragmatism marks the clinically minded (p.
169). If an intervention does not seem to work, the clinician is
likely to try something else to see if satisfactory results can be
obtained. The focus of the clinician is on the immediate and the
apparent, rather than the long range. Further, Freidson stated that
clinicians are "prone to tinker," trying successive interventions if
conventional means fail. He characterized this trial-and-error approach as crude or radical, presumably because the practitioner's
tinkering is far less refined than the systematic hypothesis testing
of the scientist.

Fourth, the clinically minded manifest a preference for relying on firsthand experience in making professional decisions,
rather than on theory or book knowledge. In professional practice,
clinical experience (one's own and that of experienced colleagues)
is placed at a premium, whereas theory and texts are devalued as

sources of knowledge. Freidson believed this generalization was especially true of clinicians attempting to manage nonroutine aspects of their work:

> Indeed, the consulting professions in general and medicine in particular encourage the limitation of perspective by its members through ideological emphasis on the importance of first-hand, individual experience and on individual freedom to make choices and to act on the basis of such experience. (p. 347)

Beyond simple prizing of clinical experience as a source of knowledge, however, Freidson asserted that practitioners tend to interpret their experience in a rather unanalytical way. Reflection and doubt are perceived to be a threat to the authority of the practitioner's gut reaction in responding quickly in highly complex situations.

Finally, clinicians tend to emphasize the "*indeterminancy or uncertainty*" (p. 169), rather than the lawfulness, of events. They are skeptical of generalizations that are supposed to hold true across cases and are likely to "express a characteristic *subjective sense* of uncertainty and vulnerability" (p. 163). Because they work with individual cases, which necessarily vary, practitioners tend to emphasize the distinctions between cases rather than their similarities. In other words, for the purposes of clinical assessment and treatment, seeing each tree and its particular features is regarded as more functional than seeing the general qualities of the forest. According to Freidson, the abstract generalizations produced through scientific research are perceived to be of limited use in the practitioner's work—one must also depend on personal clinical experience, intuition, and instinct in assessing each case. The practitioner is likely to have to "see or feel the case himself" (p. 170).

Further, the clinician is hesitant, even resistant, Freidson suggested, to change practices that appear to be getting results on the grounds of abstract considerations. Statistical findings provide limited assistance to the physician because

> medical practice is typically occupied with the problems of *individuals* rather than of aggregates or statistical units. . . . Thus, even when general scientific knowledge may be available, the mere fact of individual variability poses a constant problem for assessment that emphasizes the necessity for personal firsthand

examination of every individual case and the difficulty of disposition on some formal, abstract scientific basis. (p. 164)

While practitioners tend to reject abstract generalizations, Freidson asserted that principles of practice do evolve out of the practitioner's clinical experience, "which is to say, generalization from personal and systematically biased experience" (p. 172). This is an important point—clinicians do have theories, but their source is different than that of researchers' theories.

The preceding three qualities of clinical mentality are highly interdependent. According to Freidson, to see cases as unamenable to scientific generalizations provides a justification for a heavy reliance on personal experience as well as a pragmatic approach to decision making. As he pointed out, it is not that shared knowledge is never used, "only that thinking in terms of unique individual cases places the burden of proof on the particular rather than on the general" (p. 172).

In suggesting that practitioners maintain an unscientific perspective in clinical practice, Freidson did not wish to imply that clinicians are irrational. Clinical rationality, however, is distinct from the rationality of the scientist:

> The rationality is particularized and technical; it is a method of sorting the enormous mass of concrete detail confronting him in his individual cases. The difference between clinical rationality and scientific rationality is that clinical rationality is not a tool for the exploration or discovery of general principles, as is the scientific method, but only a tool for sorting the interconnections of perceived and hypothesized facts. (p. 171)

In other words, the task of the practitioner is to interpret a concrete case and determine what needs to be done. This sort of problem demands a different type of rationality than that which has been associated with inquiry in the natural sciences (Gatens-Robinson, 1986).

Freidson (1970) suggested that above all else, individualism and subjectivism are characteristic of the clinically minded. Each practitioner collects a private store of personal experience and beliefs and manages clients accordingly. Further, this stock of personal experience is "prone to be self-validating and self-confirming" (p. 172) because the practitioner "is so absorbed in and isolated by his own work, he is likely to see and evaluate the world more in terms of his own experience than in terms of what authorities tell him" (pp. 170–171).

Again, for the remainder of this study, the term *clinical consciousness* will be used to denote this worldview in an effort to avoid any negative connotations associated with the term *mentality*. In the next section, the discussion will turn from physicians to teachers.

CLINICAL CONSCIOUSNESS AMONG TEACHERS

Freidson's construct is useful in the educational domain because it neatly summarizes qualities of teachers' worldviews that have been revealed in both curriculum research and research on teacher thinking. Olson (1988) suggested that studies on teacher knowledge and thinking can usefully be thought of as consisting of two streams: the psychological and the epistemological. The psychological stream includes literature on how teachers plan, make decisions as they teach, and make attributions (see Clark & Peterson, 1986, for a review). Research on teachers' knowledge structures and differences between expert and novice schemata (Carter, 1988) would also fit into this category.

The epistemological stream, on the other hand, provides insight into how teachers claim to know, how they view themselves as knowers, how they understand the sources of knowledge, and how they approach problem solving. Unfortunately, most of the literature that addresses these issues tends to do so in the course of addressing a different problem, such as curriculum innovation, or is based on a very small sample or a case study of one teacher (see, for example, Clandinin, 1985; Elbaz, 1983; Jackson, 1968).

One explanation for the lack of systematic research on teachers' perspectives toward knowing is offered by Feiman-Nemser and Floden (1986), who wrote, "Teachers have not been seen as possessing a unique body of professional knowledge and expertise. The prevailing view among most researchers is that teachers have experience while academics have knowledge" (p. 512). Nevertheless, scholars have provided some highly suggestive evidence to support the claim that clinical consciousness does generally characterize the teaching occupation.

First, much evidence attests to teachers' reliance on firsthand experience in decision making (Grant & Sleeter, 1985; Hargreaves, 1984; Jackson, 1968, 1971; Lortie, 1975). In fact, Huberman (1983,

1985) asserted that teachers' firsthand experience is the crucible in which new information is tested:

> New data would appear to be tested against the accumulation of personal experience in order to judge not whether the information or expertise is valid, in some replicable manner, but whether it matches one's own generative data, whether it "fits" or "feels right." (1983, p. 481)

Firsthand experience, it would seem, provides both a justification for many teachers' decision making and a screen through which new information is filtered.

Further, based on his interviews with a sample of Chicago area teachers known for their excellence, Jackson (1968) described teachers' thinking about classroom events as highly intuitive and unanalytical:

> The unquestioning acceptance of classroom miracles is part of a broader tendency that reveals itself in several ways in the talk of teachers. This is the tendency to approach educational affairs intuitively rather than rationally. When called on to justify their professional decisions, for example, my informants often declared that their classroom behavior was based more on impulse and feeling than on reflection and thought. (p. 145)

Jackson noted that despite this intuitive and unreflective approach to their work, teachers tend to assert their beliefs about teaching with tenacity:

> Like amateur art-lovers they knew what they liked, even if they did not always know why they liked it. When pressed for a rationalization of their pedagogical tastes they not infrequently became impatient or hid behind the defense of *de gustibus non est disputandum*. Rarely, if ever, did they turn to evidence beyond their own personal experience to justify their professional preferences. (p. 146)

Jackson's interviews support the claim that teachers tend to be confident, subjective, and individualistic in their professional views.

In addition, some researchers have described teachers as pragmatic in their decision making (Doyle & Ponder, 1977–1978; Lortie, 1975) and intuitive in their approach to problem solving

(Doyle & Ponder, 1977–1978; Jackson, 1968, 1971; Lortie, 1975). Doyle and Ponder referred to the pragmatic elements in teacher decision making as the "practicality ethic." Based on their survey of curriculum innovation literature, they concluded that teachers rapidly label proposals for change as "practical" or "impractical" based on their estimations of the probable consequences of implementing an innovation in their classroom. Similarly, Bolster (1983) wrote, "teachers' knowledge of teaching is validated pragmatically. Principles are believed to be true when they give rise to actions that 'work'" (p. 298). Lortie (1975), in his interviews with teachers, found that "the criterion of suitability to self is supplemented by a pragmatism of a highly personal sort. The practice must work 'for me,' and the teacher is the judge of what works" (p. 78). This research also points to a highly subjective and individualistic view of teaching practice. Not only is whether something works subjectively assessed, but the suitability of any innovation is seen to hinge on the personality and preferences of the individual teacher.

Also, supporting the claim that teachers are generally particularistic in their thinking, they have been found to be skeptical about, or uninterested in, generalizations (Bolster, 1983; Huberman, 1983, 1985; Jackson 1971). Doyle and Ponder (1977–1978) also suggested that teachers tend to emphasize the uniqueness of each classroom.

Huberman (1983) characterized teachers' orientation toward knowledge and problem solving in the following way:

> The global image emerging from the classic and recent studies of knowledge use by teachers is that of practically oriented professionals drawing chiefly on their own and their peers' experience to resolve problems or otherwise modify their instructional practices. Recourse to more scientific, distant, or noneducational sources is infrequent. . . . There is a good deal of recipe collecting and exchanging, enabling teachers to expand their instructional repertoire, their bag of tricks. These recipes are traded on the basis of a validation that is craft embedded and highly experiential; ideas, techniques, products, and explanations of classroom life that "worked for me" are circulated among users, but undergo an intuitive test—how the message or product feels or fits—before being tried out in the classroom. (pp. 483–484)

This research indicates that clinical consciousness is characteristic of at least a significant portion of teachers. Other researchers have also found Freidson's construct useful in this domain (Hogben, 1982; Sergiovanni, 1985).

In recent years, Huberman (1983), Jackson (1968), and Lortie (1975) have been criticized on the grounds that they embrace a view of practice that emanates from positivism (Copa, 1991) and an unjustifiably dim view of teacher thinking (Clark & Lampert, 1985; see also Feiman-Nemser & Floden, 1986). These critiques do not challenge the descriptive accuracy of their work, but rather the value judgments that Huberman, Jackson, and Lortie place on their findings. Copa attributed these disparaging conclusions about teacher thinking to Lortie's and Jackson's apparent disappointment that teachers fail to conform to a top-down technical approach to practice:

> The theory that the experienced teachers in this literature "lacked" was a form that is viewed as existing apart from and actually transcending experience and action—particularly as these elements are encountered in particular instances. . . . Because mastery and use of universal laws are considered necessary for predicting and ultimately controlling the social as well as the physical environment . . . , when teachers do not reflect "proper" application of these formalized laws in their pure forms, the educators' conceptual functioning, as well as the effectiveness of their actions, may be—and often have been—questioned. (p. 112)

To have a dim view of these findings on teacher thinking does not require a devotion to positivism: it simply requires a commitment to the idea that educational research has something to contribute to practice. The teachers Jackson interviewed did not simply lack the "mastery and use of universal laws"—they saw research as largely irrelevant to their work. The concerns of Huberman, Jackson, and Lortie about teachers and their ways of thinking may or may not reflect their adherence to positivistic conceptions of practice.

Clark and Lampert (1985) argued that teachers' intuitive, present-oriented, and even irrational thinking should be understood as adaptive to or functional in practice, rather than as grounds for criticism. They wrote, "Instead of seeing all these features as limitations of teachers, we now understand that they are appropriate and essential for getting the job done" (p. 7). Again, Clark and Lampert are not quarreling with the descriptions that Jackson, Lortie, and others forward, but with how such assertions should be interpreted. Yet, functional and adaptive modes of practice do not facilitate transformative inquiry and action. Thus, if "getting the job done" includes any kind of transformative role for the teacher, then these qualities are only partially appropriate for practice.

In keeping with Freidson (1970), the following discussion will explore the conditions of teaching as a source of clinical consciousness. It will be suggested that teachers, like the physicians of Freidson's study, work in a context that may well promote this perspective.

THE CONDITIONS OF TEACHING

It is Freidson's (1970) contention that the worldview he found to be common among everyday physicians is related to the demands and contingencies of practice:

> One whose work requires practical application to concrete cases simply cannot maintain the same frame of mind as the scholar or scientist: he cannot suspend action in the absence of incontrovertible evidence or be skeptical of himself, his experience, his work and its fruit. In emergencies he cannot wait for the discoveries of the future. Dealing with individual cases, he cannot rely solely on probabilities or on general concepts or principles: he must also rely on his own senses. By the nature of his work the clinician must assume responsibility for practical action, and in doing so he must rely on his concrete, clinical experience. (pp. 169–170)

Extrapolating from Freidson's analysis, it is plausible to infer that clinical consciousness is more likely to be characteristic of some practitioners than of others.

The following discussion will explore the context of teaching as a source of clinical consciousness. Teachers, like the physicians in Freidson's study, work in a setting that may foster clinical consciousness. In fact, the nature of teachers' working conditions may even promote it to a greater extent than the physician's workplace. Researchers such as Doyle (1979), Dreeben (1973), Feiman-Nemser and Floden (1986), Jackson (1968, 1971, 1986), and Lortie (1975) have described in great detail the nature of the conditions of teaching. Their analyses reveal that teachers, like everyday physicians, generally work in an occupational context that is characterized by continual demands for action, pervasive ambiguity, relative isolation, and a heterogeneous clientele. This is not to say that all teaching contexts are identical (Feiman-Nemser & Floden, 1986; Rosenholtz, 1985, 1989), but that these general conditions are dominant in the occupation.

Pressure to Act

Some practitioners must routinely intervene at a moment's notice: their concrete problems are characterized by a high degree of pressure to act. The practice of emergency room physicians, for example, involves cases of inordinate urgency. Other practices, however, are marked by cases requiring far less immediate action on the part of the practitioner. Physicians who specialize in internal medicine, for example, are well-known for running laboratory tests and conferring with colleagues before making a diagnosis, thus delaying action until all the results are in.

Similarly, the architect and the engineer can usually delay action. Like the physician, these practitioners apply their expertise to the solution of concrete problems; yet, their cases do not require immediate action. They can usually put the problem down until later with no ill effects; they may even tear up the first draft of a solution if they choose and try again for a better outcome. Practitioners working under conditions of low pressure may even reformulate or reframe the problem itself. In short, one way in which professions vary is the pressure for action that cases impose on practitioners: how quickly must the clinician generally act in this case or that?

It stands to reason that practitioners who work under conditions of high demand for action would tend to manifest not only an orientation to taking action, but also a reliance on firsthand experience as a source of knowledge. Under such conditions, there is little time to consult books or colleagues, or to gather data. In addition, gut instinct and an intuitive grasp of cases are likely to be prized and honed.

Teaching has often been characterized as a practice of high demand for taking action. A useful way to conceptualize this particular aspect of the teacher's role is posited by Westbury (1973). In its most general form, he suggested, teaching necessarily entails the performance of three tasks:

1. The presentation of subject-matter content
2. The provision of opportunities for students to rehearse the content to be learned

3. The creation of an environment that enhances student motivation to engage in the teacher's activities

This generic model, according to Westbury, holds for all teaching,
from the tutorial to the conventional classroom.

The classroom setting, however, makes teaching a far more
complicated enterprise:

> The classroom does not alter the essential character of these
> teaching tasks, but it makes their execution more complex: a
> classroom has numbers of students who are at different states
> of readiness for the particular learning at hand, have different
> ability levels, different enthusiasms, and, inevitably, differing
> willingnesses to attend, here and now, to this particular topic.
> (Westbury, 1973, p. 111)

While there is no doubt that the heterogeneity of an average class
of children makes the accomplishment of the three tasks cited
above difficult, the more important consequence of the classroom
setting is that it requires the teacher to be a manager of children,
time, and resources. Thus, by virtue of teaching in a crowded setting, the teacher's role is expanded to include a fourth task: classroom management (Westbury, 1973).

The task of classroom management consists primarily of
maintaining order among 20 to 40 children in a small crowded
space in which "scattered events can arise from unexpected quar-
ters at unexpected times" (Dreeben, 1973, p. 461). Teachers must
be constantly alert to the possibility of disruption and its sources
and maintain what Kounin (1972) called "with-itness." Otherwise,
they risk having their instructional activities subverted. Contributing to the pressure for action imposed by this task is the fact that
students are "conscripts," required to attend classes until the age
of 16. On the other hand, teachers have no legal power to select
their clients (Lortie, 1975). Another factor is the students' youth:
school children are only partially socialized and therefore not prepared to work on any one task for a prolonged period of time (Lortie, 1975). Thus, children are prone to go off task and engage in
disruptive behavior. The point here is that while the teacher provides instruction either to the whole group or to individuals, he or
she must at the same time keep a watchful eye on the entire group.

Teaching in a crowded setting also adds other duties to the
previous ones: the teacher must keep track of time, monitor discussions, and oversee the distribution and use of classroom mate-

rials (Jackson, 1968). This quality of teaching, which requires the monitoring of several activities at once, prompted Smith and Geoffrey (1968) to liken the teacher's role to that of a "circus ringmaster" (p. 104). Perhaps Jackson (1971) put it best when he wrote:

> When the occasions for action come and go in a twinkling there is little opportunity for careful reasoning and debate. While the teacher is thinking about how to answer one student's question, three others raise their hands. Just as he bends over to examine a student's workbook, a commotion breaks out at the side of the room. In the midst of reading a story to the class, he suddenly remembers that the student he sent on an errand fifteen minutes ago has not yet returned. And so it goes. The pressure for quick and decisive action is constantly upon the teacher. (p. 28)

A final point regarding Westbury's model is that the four tasks of teaching often compete with each other. If content is covered at a brisk pace, the provision of opportunities for students to rehearse the content must be sacrificed. If a teacher moves too slowly through the text in an effort to maximize the chance for everyone to learn the content, he or she risks additional management difficulties. The greater the emphasis on order and discipline, the more difficult it is to maintain motivation. When motivation wanes, it is more difficult to gain compliance in instructional activities, and then coverage and mastery suffer. It is because of these tensions that much of the teacher's behavior can be conceived of as coping behavior, the outcome of an attempt to meet the task demands of teaching (Westbury, 1973; see also Lampert, 1985). Interestingly enough, Shulman (1987) asserted, "The only time a physician could possibly encounter a situation of comparable complexity would be in the emergency room of a hospital during or after a natural disaster" (p. 376).

Based on this analysis, it is reasonable to characterize teaching as a practice of high pressure for action; therefore, it is expected that teachers may be likely to manifest an orientation to action and a prizing of firsthand experience and intuition, rather than analysis and reflection.

Ambiguity

Practices vary according to the degree of uncertainty or ambiguity clinicians must face. This ambiguity may stem in part from the nature of the clinician's task. For example, Gatens-Robinson

(1986) wrote that the physician typically faces "ill-structured" tasks that "resemble those that occur during periods of epistemological crisis" (p. 170). She continued:

> In such circumstances, neither the presenting problem nor the goal of the reasoning process are defined in advance. That definition constitutes part of the task itself. This domain of the ill-structured problem seems to describe the epistemological terrain of much of clinical judgment. It is the situation that the physician faces with each new patient. (p. 170)

Not only may there be uncertainty about the nature of the problem itself, but also about how to deal with it. This uncertainty may stem from the limits of the professional knowledge base, incomplete mastery of available knowledge, or the difficulty of distinguishing between the two (Fox, 1957). It may be expected that clinicians who practice under conditions of extreme ambiguity would have to maintain faith in the efficacy of their own actions as a requisite to practice.

The uncertainties and ambiguities of teaching have been a theme of many scholarly papers in recent years (Floden & Clark, 1988; Jackson, 1968, 1986). Structural factors in the occupation make various types of uncertainty endemic to the teacher's work (Lortie, 1975). In the previous section, teaching was characterized as a practice that demands constant action taking. Those actions must frequently be taken under the conditions of epistemological crisis, conditions noted by Gatens-Robinson (1986) to be characteristic of the physician's work. The teacher has to constantly pick up cues, read children's faces, and remain "with-it" (Kounin, 1972) to be able to interpret what is occurring in the classroom. In short, there is not only pressure to act, but frequently the problems facing the teacher are "ill-structured."

There are other sources of uncertainty as well. For example, several factors hinder teachers' efforts to gauge the success of their actions (Lortie, 1975). First, as stated above, teachers must balance four tasks that often compete with each other. Success in one realm may mean weaker performance in the others. As Lortie (1975) pointed out, there is no single dimension upon which teachers' performance can be assessed. Thus, the teacher may be a good classroom manager, but poor at meeting instructional goals. To the extent that goals are not set at the organizational level, teachers may have little recourse but to develop their own criteria of success and failure.

Further, uncertainty is compounded by the fact that teachers produce no tangible product (Jackson, 1986). Unlike engineers, architects, or auto workers, they cannot point to a product as evidence that they have accomplished something or made a difference. Unlike other workers who receive immediate feedback, frequently teachers must send children off to the next grade level not knowing whether their labors have paid off.

Finally, the teacher's influence on any student's learning is mitigated by a variety of factors that undercut the ability of the teacher to attribute student progress directly to his or her instructional efforts. The influence of the home is probably the most powerful of these factors. Indeed, to the extent that students are viewed as responsible for their own learning, the teacher's ability to take credit for student success is compromised.

Thus, a teacher's uncertainty about the efficacy of his or her actions stems from the multidimensional quality of teaching, the lack of a tangible product, and the unclear lines of influence. In the absence of any concrete measure of their success, it is anticipated that teachers generally tend to have faith that their efforts produce valuable outcomes and that their actions are sound in order to continue to practice.

Isolation

Some practitioners work in cooperative or collaborative settings, whereas others work in relative isolation. Where work is conducted largely in isolation, the individualistic perspective that is characteristic of clinical consciousness may flourish because the practitioner is primarily reliant on his or her own clinical experience and senses in treating cases and there is little check on subjective interpretation (see Scriven, 1979). Where colleagues share responsibility for a client, it may be far more difficult to develop the "self-validating and self-confirming" (p. 172) perspective Freidson described.

Perhaps the single most important organizational quality of schools is their cellular or "egg crate" structure (Lortie, 1975, p. 14). In most schools, despite innovations such as team teaching, the norm is that teachers work in isolation behind their individual classroom doors (Lortie, 1975; Rosenholtz, 1989). This spatial separation signifies that teachers generally have few opportunities to see colleagues teach and cannot offer advice (or get assistance) on the basis of direct observation. Dreeben (1973) noted, "This is not to deny that teachers talk shop and talk about each other's problems; they cannot do so, however, on the basis of shared visible and audible experiences" (p. 469). Thus, advice from colleagues has a secondhand quality to it. Further, those administrators who generally carry the responsibility for teacher supervision generally have little time to devote to the task of formative evaluation (Raths, 1982). As a consequence, Dreeben (1973) termed teaching a "very solitary and private kind of work" (p. 469).

The reward structure of the occupation reinforces the teacher's isolation. Generally, because of long traditions in teaching, individuals who seek financial gain and high status do not enter the occupation. Instead, psychic benefits have been found to be an important incentive to teachers. Data suggest that the source of psychic rewards for most teachers is related to successful outcomes with students (Lortie, 1975). If teachers accrue psychic rewards primarily through effort expended in the classroom, as opposed to activities at the building level, it stands to reason that this spatial separation will be reinforced as they concentrate on teaching activities (Lortie, 1975).

In addition, novice teachers are socialized and inducted into the profession under conditions of isolation. Teacher candidates rarely are placed in cohorts or visit classrooms as groups to collaborate over shared observations. During the student teaching practicum, each candidate is usually assigned to one teacher, who works independently. The novice teacher is then expected to take on independently the same responsibilities as a veteran. In what Lortie (1975) termed the "sink or swim" phenomenon, the neophyte generally must assume these duties without opportunities for help from more experienced colleagues:

> When his untutored eye identifies a difficulty, he may request help. But there is a secondhand quality to such assistance: if the advisor is not someone who regularly visits the classroom, the teacher must describe the situation. The advisor may offer suggestions, but the beginner must attempt a solution and decide on his own whether it has sufficed. The beginner's perceptions and interpersonal skills mediate between external advice and classroom events; his learning is limited by his personal resources—the acuity of his observation and his capacity to take effective action. (p. 73)

Teachers, largely independently, must rely on their own skills, talents, and intuition in learning how to teach.

In summary, the fact that teachers work under isolated conditions and are socialized and inducted into those arrangements would tend to foster a reliance on firsthand experience and a pragmatic stance in meeting problems of practice.

Variability

Some practices involve work with materials that are roughly homogeneous whereas other practices, such as the human service professions, do not. At one extreme, a practitioner may work with materials that are extremely similar from sample to sample. Carpenters, for example, work with certain types of wood that are more or less constant in quality: oak has certain qualities, whereas teak and pine have others (Diorio, 1982). Under these kinds of conditions, it is possible to have extensive knowledge of the qualities of the materials with which one is working and know that under certain conditions the materials will behave in a specific way.

At the other extreme, practitioners work under conditions in which individual variation and reaction are a constant challenge. For the physician, an antibiotic that works for the first patient may fail the second; the therapies that cured one patient may contribute nothing to the treatment of another. In addition, these variable qualities are largely unpredictable. It is very likely that these conditions contribute to a distrust of generalizations, a sense of the lack of an underlying order, and a tendency to emphasize the indeterminancy of events.

A salient quality of teaching practice is the individual variability of students. Working with students is not like working with wood or metals (Diorio, 1982). Students are heterogeneous and reactive to any number of factors, which precludes the possibility of predicting with certainty whether a given activity is going to be received well or not:

> Interaction effects may vary from situation to situation, and across settings, so that inferences drawn from earlier experience may not apply to this case. Teachers frequently are uncertain as to how to proceed. Their uncertainty is exacerbated by another feature of the teaching-learning process: the actual—as opposed to the intended—consequences of practices depend on how these particular students, at this moment, perceive and construe them. (Sanders & McCutcheon, 1986, p. 53)

In other words, a teacher may give the same lesson twice in one day to find overwhelming success one time and blank stares the next:

> The techniques that work well with one student fail with the next, the well-prepared lesson falls flat and the *ad lib* activity is an unqualified (and unexpected) success, the discussion that was dragging along for several minutes suddenly, for no apparent reason, comes to life. (Jackson, 1971, p. 18)

Further, the intervening variables are largely unknowable to the teacher. Unlike scientists, teachers do not have the luxury of testing treatments under controlled experimental conditions. Although this quality of teaching practice no doubt contributes to the uncertainty of teachers' work, it is a special type of uncertainty that extends beyond the dilemma of interpretation and action described previously. Working under such conditions, it is reasonable to assert, would foster a particularistic stance and a skepticism toward, if not a disdain of, abstract generalizations. Huberman (1983) explained:

> If outcomes are largely unpredictable or often noncontingent on what a teacher does or doesn't do in the classroom, practitioners are likely to spend little time reasoning about their practice or listening to others who employ a logical, scientific, or detached perspective. (p. 497)

In short, the generalizations of scientific research are not compatible with the seemingly haphazard nature of classroom events.

This analysis suggests that the task demands and conditions of teaching promote clinical consciousness. These factors include the pressure for taking immediate action, the ambiguity associated with both interpretation and action, the isolation, and a variable clientele. In addition, it is important to note that teachers and the practice of teaching are nested in a wider cultural setting. Elements of clinical consciousness have historically received wide ideological support in our culture.

IDEOLOGICAL INFLUENCES

Social scientists and men of letters have long noted that one of the most powerful strains of American ideology rails against theorists and book learning in favor of common sense and intuition. Ralph Waldo Emerson wrote in his journals during Jackson's presidency:

> Because our education is defective, because we are superficial and ill-read, we are forced to make the most of that position, of ignorance. Hence America is a vast know-nothing party, and we disparage books, and cry up intuition. With a few clever men we have made a reputable thing of that, and denouncing libraries and severe culture, and magnifying the mother-wit swagger of bright boys from the country colleges, we have even come so far as to deceive everybody, except ourselves, into an admiration of unlearning and inspiration, forsooth. (cited in Beale, 1936, p. 652)

Tocqueville also noted the American impatience with careful study and reflection in his essays written in the 1830s. He wrote that "men who live in democratic communities not only seldom indulge in meditation, but they naturally entertain very little esteem for it" (cited in Borrowman, 1956, p. 32).

A century later, Beale (1936) stated in his study of American teachers and freedom:

> The American people have brought down from pioneer days a profound respect for the practical, and a distrust of "mere theorists" . . . even Americans who are suffering from the inequities of the rules of the business game look for better times to the very men who are responsible for those inequities, and distrust and fear the theories of reformers and theorists. (p. 649)

Even when it is not in the interest of individuals to align with "practical men," Beale suggested, Americans prefer that alternative to siding with theorists.

Buchmann and Schwille (1983) pointed out that the prevalence of aphorisms such as "live and learn," "see for yourself," and "seeing is believing" reinforces this bias against book learning and toward firsthand experience as a source of knowledge. As a culture, we deride individuals who are "bookish" and chide ourselves not to believe everything we read. Nisbett and Ross (1980) noted:

> Although people seem to be aware that the senses may mislead ("Your eyes can play tricks on you"), there seems to be little recognition that concrete information, even if perceived correctly, still can generate incorrect inferences. What is needed, perhaps,

is a new set of prescriptive homilies of the following type: "Just because it's punchy doesn't mean it's important," "Yes, it's interesting, but what does it prove?" or "Don't try to use a 'man-who' statistic on me." (p. 61)

Perhaps the most famous study of this phenomenon is Hofstadter's (1963) work, *Anti-Intellectualism in American Life*. Hofstadter argued that "the belief in mass education was not founded primarily upon a passion for the development of mind, or upon pride in learning and culture for their own sakes, but rather upon the supposed political and economic benefits of education" (p. 305). Key examples of school reform efforts hinged on rationales other than the intrinsic value of education can be found as early as the writings of Benjamin Rush and as recently as the 1983 U.S. Department of Education report, *A Nation at Risk*.

Wiebe (1984), a social historian, suggested that Americans' anti-intellectualism stems in part from the experience of settling a frontier nation. This experience involved constant pressure to take action under conditions of uncertainty:

> The guiding principle of the universe, Henry Ward Beecher declared, was "the law of growth," and growth in the early 19th century forced all units of society into the pressure box of incessant responses to incessant changes. (Wiebe, 1984, p. 286)

The pressure for economic growth on the frontier in the 1800s, Wiebe argued, gave rise to "parallelism," a particular kind of individualism, particularism, and subjectivism. Parallelism, as he defined it, was the "assumption that each social unit had a right to its own testing lane. There it would pit its special inner qualities, its distinctive application of the truth, against the challenges of progress" (p. 287). Each city or town, in its race for development, had its own unique experience and it was therefore believed that "a failure elsewhere had no necessary application whatsoever to its own try" (p. 287). According to Wiebe, one result of parallelism was a susceptibility to fads that had been demonstrated again and again as failures.

This analysis, which is only meant to be suggestive, supports the idea that elements of clinical consciousness are endemic to our culture as a whole. Teachers working in the type of setting described above are likely to have their clinical consciousness reinforced, rather than challenged, in our culture.

CONCLUSION

In this chapter, Freidson's construct, clinical mentality, referred to here as clinical consciousness, has been introduced and applied to the field of teaching. It has been argued that this concept aptly characterizes the worldview of many teachers and that one of clinical consciousness's sources is found in teachers' classroom experience. Specifically, the pressures of teaching a heterogeneous clientele in an isolated setting under conditions of uncertainty have been related to a clinical worldview. Elements of clinical consciousness, it was argued, are broadly supported in our culture at large. In the next chapter, the analysis will expand beyond the work context to describe another possible source of clinical consciousness that complements Freidson's (1970) analysis; namely, that the perspective he described may be, in part, a developmental perspective.

2

A Developmental Perspective of Clinical Consciousness

The practice of teaching no doubt writes upon teachers; however, it is also true that teachers do not enter the occupation as blank slates. Teaching itself is shaped by the understandings and perspectives individuals bring to their practice. Whereas Freidson offered a sociological explanation of clinical consciousness, a study by Belenky, Clinchy, Goldberger, and Tarule (1986) suggests that clues to its source may also be found in developmental processes. Their research, extending the work of Perry (1970), Gilligan (1982), and others, examined how women from various social class backgrounds and age groups view knowledge and its sources and perceive themselves as knowers and problem solvers. The interview data revealed to the authors five basic "ways of knowing," which represent different solutions to the problem of integrating reason and emotion. They maintain that many women find this integration exceedingly difficult to achieve and that it is poorly facilitated in most formal educational settings. It is reasonable to believe that this synthesis is generally problematic for men as well; however, the focus of Belenky et al.'s work is on women's epistemological development.

Women's Ways of Knowing is particularly provocative for teacher education, a field that historically has served primarily women. Belenky et al.'s research provides a theoretical framework for discussing clinical consciousness in the context of other orientations toward knowing and provides insight into the type of teaching that might foster the intellectual growth of women. This chapter will summarize these findings and their implications in relationship to clinical consciousness and teacher education. Before describing the ways of knowing delineated by Belenky et al., however, a brief introduction to their research will be provided.

EARLIER RESEARCH ON EPISTEMOLOGICAL DEVELOPMENT

Perry's (1970) study of the epistemological development of college-age men is an important forerunner to Belenky's et al.'s work. Perry, a cognitive developmental psychologist, interviewed undergraduates at Harvard College in the 1950s and early 1960s. That study (Perry, 1970) uncovered nine positions from which men viewed the nature of knowledge, truth, and authority. Perry's findings provided Belenky et al. (1986) with their "first images of the paths women might take as they developed an understanding of their intellectual potential" (p. 10).

Perry posited a linear sequence of developmental perspectives or "positions," which he defined as coherent frameworks for interpreting experience. In Perry's scheme, development proceeds from an initial position of basic duality, in which the world is conceived of in black or white, right or wrong terms. Knowledge is accumulated from authorities through hard work and conformity. As the student is confronted with a diversity of conflicting opinion, he is pressed to move beyond dualism to multiplicity. In multiplicity, a student recognizes uncertainty or gray areas, and adopts a "you have your opinion, I have mine" stance. Disputes between authorities are taken to be conflicts of personal preferences, and the student is at a loss to arbitrate between points of view. Finally, as students are pressed to defend their opinions with evidence and reasons, they move to a position of relativism, in which all knowledge is taken to be constructed, contextual, and tentative. It is this perspective through which individuals develop responsibility and informed commitment, according to Perry. This sequence of development, although linear, can be interrupted or arrested if an individual finds growth too painful or threatening; for example, it is possible that individuals can remain in a dualistic or multiplistic position indefinitely (Belenky et al., 1986).

Although Perry's research has been highly influential, its generalizability is compromised in a number of ways. It is limited by its focus upon men and, in particular, elite men. Issues of race, class, and gender are virtually ignored in his study. This observation points to Gilligan's contributions to psychological theory because her work (1982) is in large part an attempt to redress the masculine bias of traditional psychology research conducted by researchers such as Perry and Kohlberg (1981).

Gilligan argued that traditional psychological research established men's experience as a standard against which female experience is evaluated. For example, Kohlberg advanced a theory of cognitive moral development based on studies of men and boys. In her research, Gilligan found that women develop an ethic of responsibility and care, rather than the morality of autonomy and rights that Kohlberg found in men. For Belenky et al. (1986), Gilligan's work highlighted the need to listen to women talk about their experience independent of constructs based on studies of men.

Aside from addressing the issue of gender, Belenky et al. extended Perry's research in other ways. Perry studied a group of relatively homogeneous elite men undergoing a socialization experience in a particular milieu. Belenky et al. asserted that the relative uniformity of Perry's sample and the common experience the participants were undergoing contributed to the linearity of Perry's developmental sequence (p. 15). By contrast, Belenky and her colleagues interviewed women of different ages, social class backgrounds, and ethnic groups who brought their various life experiences to the study.

WOMEN'S WAYS OF KNOWING

The study reported in *Women's Ways of Knowing* is based on interviews with 135 students and non-career women, aged 16 to 65, selected from nine sites, ranging from an elite women's college to family agencies that serve women and their children. Thus, the study included women who were advantaged and disadvantaged, from rural and urban settings. Through intensive interviews, Belenky and her coauthors uncovered five basic epistemological positions from which women view the world. These five "ways of knowing" are the different ways that women view knowledge, authority, and truth and they are intimately linked with the issues of self-worth and psychological connection.

The authors caution that these perspectives are not fixed or discrete, nor do they account for the complexity of women's thinking. Belenky et al. (1986) are hesitant to call the perspectives they describe "stages." They wrote, "We describe in this book epistemological *perspectives* from which women know and view the world. We leave it to future work to determine whether these perspectives have any stagelike qualities" (p. 15). Although Perry's data showed a clearer line of development for men at Harvard than this study does for women, Belenky et al. (1986) suggested, as noted above, that an explanation for the clarity of that path can be found in the homogeneity of the study's sample and the common experience of the male undergraduates at Harvard. Yet, through the interviews, the authors were able to speculate as to the paths that shifts in position might follow.

Finally, Belenky and her co-authors point out that these orientations do not exclusively characterize women: similar orientations can be found in men's thinking as well. Thus, the five epistemological perspectives described below cannot be taken to be exclusively characteristic of women. How Belenky et al.'s findings differ from those of Perry (1970) will be addressed following a summary of the five ways of knowing.

Silence

The first epistemological perspective, silence, is a position in which women believe themselves to be basically incapable of knowing anything important. Silent women, according to the authors, "experience themselves as mindless and voiceless and subject to the whims of external authority" (p. 15). One of the salient characteristics of silent women is that they fail to develop the capacity for representational thought. Because language and words remain alien to them, sharing in the social life of the community or reflecting on their own experience is extremely difficult. Thus, silent women tend to remain alienated both from themselves and from others. In short, these women tend to feel powerless, dependent, and silent. Belenky et al. attribute this perspective to growing up in circumstances of extreme deprivation and often family violence. Few of the subjects in the study's sample could be classified in this category.

Received Knowing

The second perspective is received knowing, in which women believe that what is true or what they know must come from external sources. Knowledge for women who hold this perspective is created by other people and received from them. Furthermore, they are dualistic in their thinking, seeing things in either/or terms. Thus, received knowers tend to be uncomfortable with ambiguity:

> They have trouble with poetry. It is not clear to them why poets do not just say right out what they mean. Literature is full of equivocation, and they do not see why this is so. They are *literal*. . . . They like predictability. . . . They like clarity. They want to know exactly what they are expected to do. (p. 42)

Belenky et al. suggested that students with this orientation will be the ones to ask how grades will be calculated and how many pages the term paper must be.

Unlike silent women, received knowers are capable of learning, but learning consists of mastering what authorities or experts have said. The authors noted that the women in the study who held this perspective tended to be just starting their college careers or participating in one of the social service agencies that served as a site for the study. Belenky and her colleagues wrote that for women to manifest this perspective at latter stages of their college careers was uncommon because an academic environment usually challenges it.

Subjective Knowing

The third perspective, especially relevant to the analysis of clinical consciousness, is subjective knowing. This orientation, the authors maintained, is as authoritarian as the received-knowing perspective, but now the source of truth is the individual's gut feeling, personal experience, and intuition (Belenky et al., 1986). Significantly, Belenky et al. reported that nearly half of the women they interviewed were predominantly subjectivist in orientation. The authors noted, "They appeared in every educational and agency setting included in the study. They cut across class, ethnic, age, and educational boundaries" (p. 55). Because of the commonalities between the subjectivist perspective and clinical consciousness, their findings about this orientation will be discussed at length.

The subjectivist position, the researchers found, includes a faith in personal experience and gut instinct as a source of truth and a repudiation of experts:

> Although so-called experts may have done more thinking on a subject, subjectivists feel that they don't have to accept what the experts say. Another person's opinion may be misguided or disagreeable; but they have a tolerance for differences, since oth-

ers "must obviously believe in their opinion." (Belenky et al., 1986, p. 70)

The findings of experts or scholars are simply other opinions based on different experience. This prizing of firsthand experience and intuition is accompanied by a distrust of books as a source of knowledge. Because subjectivists reject texts that contradict their own experience, they often have a difficult time in school as they pit their firsthand experience against texts. Thus, Belenky et al. stated that university faculty often find subjective knowers difficult because they tend not to be susceptible to compelling arguments or data beyond their own experience.

The authors found that subjectivists frequently rejected science and scientists. These women, the authors wrote, drew sharp distinctions between their own way of knowing, which was largely intuitive, and the logic and abstraction of the scientist. Interestingly enough, the authors observed that this rejection of theory and analysis was not itself the result of any reasoned assessment of intuition versus analytic thinking. Rather, their repudiation of scientific inquiry seemed itself to be largely emotive, based on "untested prejudices against a mode of thought that they sense ... may be detrimental to their capacity for feeling" (p. 71). For example, one subjective knower in the study dismissed theory as "intellectualism" (p. 73).

Another characteristic of subjectivist women is pragmatism, a focus on what "works" or "feels right":

> When faced with controversy, subjectivist women become strictly pragmatic—"what works best for me." They refer back to the centrality of their personal experience, whether they are talking about right choices for themselves or others. They insist that, since everyone's experience is unique, no one has the right to speak for others or to judge what others have to say. (p. 70)

This perspective embraces not only a crude empiricism and pragmatism, but also an element of particularism. These women are in effect saying that one has to experience the problem firsthand in order to know what to do.

What prompted these women into a subjectivist position? Belenky et al. stated that the histories of subjectivist women, both the affluent and unprivileged, include elements of failed or rejected male authority or both. For example, Belenky and her co-authors found that women who had been abused finally left their husbands on the strength of their feelings and found new strength through that experience. Similarly, they reported that middle-class women, socialized to be pleasing and obedient to family and to society at large, rejected that role in order to find themselves. In sum, a path for many women seemed to be the shift from the received-knowing position to the subjectivist position, as reliance on others' knowledge was found to be disappointing, unaccept-able, or stifling. Subjectivist women reject the received-knowledge orientation—sometimes in periods of crisis—and begin to look to themselves, although in an authoritarian way, as a source of knowledge. The authors noted that frequently the shift from received knowing to subjective knowing is the result of a particular episode or interaction:

> The point at which individual women begin to express negative attitudes toward abstraction, theory, and science differs from person to person, although in many cases it is anchored in a concrete interaction with a specific teacher or doctor or male acquaintance from the past. Some of the young students we interviewed recalled their frustration with a particular instructor; mothers often looked back on their struggle with a doctor over the proper treatment for a child. (p. 72)

Often, the transition is supported by other women with similar experiences in self-help groups, by social service agencies, or by family members. This discussion will return to subjectivism—and its relationship to clinical consciousness—after the final two orientations are described below.

Procedural Knowing

Whereas subjective knowing is characterized by a turning inward to find the truth, individuals who are procedural knowers believe that knowledge is the outcome of a process requiring careful observation and analysis. Thus, these individuals believe that no one's intuition is unsusceptible to error. Belenky and her co-authors found that for these women, form predominated over content, methodology over substance.

An important aspect of procedural knowing is the notion of perspective-taking, or "ways of looking":

The notion of "ways of looking" is central to the procedural knowledge position. It builds upon the subjectivist insight that different people have—and have a right to have—different opinions. . . . They believe that each of us looks at the world through a different lens, that each of us construes the world differently. They are interested not just in *what* people think but in *how* people go about forming their opinions and feelings and ideas. (p. 97)

As opposed to subjectivists, procedural knowers strive for a certain degree of objectivity, for seeing all sides of an issue.

Belenky et al. distinguished between separate and connected procedural knowing. Separate procedural knowing involves the implementation of interpersonal rules or processes. Connected knowing entails learning to adopt another person's viewpoint through the process of empathy or caring. All procedural knowing, however, is focused away from the self to an object or another person:

Separate knowers learn through explicit formal instruction how to adopt a different lens—how, for example, to think like a sociologist. Connected knowers learn through empathy. Both learn to get out from behind their own eyes and use a different lens, in one case the lens of a discipline, in the other the lens of another person. (p. 115)

In other words, separate knowers attempt to use, for example, scientific procedures to circumvent the perceived limitations and biases of subjective knowing. Connected knowers, on the other hand, do not so much try to filter personal bias out, as identify or empathize with another person's experience in order to augment their own understanding.

Separate and connected knowing differ in one more important respect. Separate knowers are doubters. These individuals examine arguments to look for flaws and loopholes and are skeptical of what others say, although they are willing to listen to the sound arguments of others. There is an adversarial dimension to separate knowing. In contrast, connected knowers hold off criticism and doubt. They seek to understand the positions of others, which requires the suspension of disbelief: they are willing, at least temporarily, to give credibility to the points of view of others.

Belenky et al. (1986) maintained that part of this willingness of connected procedural knowers to suspend judgment comes from the subjectivist view that all beliefs come from experience and personal experience cannot be wrong; yet, unlike subjectivists, connected knowers can open up beyond their own truths. The authors describe the connected knowing orientation in the following way:

> Sometimes, but not always, a woman adopts another person's ideas as her own. Through empathy she expands her experiential base; she acquires vicarious (secondhand, firsthand) experience and so expands her knowledge. (p. 115)

Thus, it seems important for procedural knowers to understand how ideas and points of view evolved, as well as the content of the ideas themselves.

Belenky and colleagues wrote that almost all of the women in their sample who became procedural knowers were once subjectivists or received knowers. One of the factors that seemed to foster this shift in orientation was the experience of situations and contexts in which subjectivism and received knowing were challenged. For example, they recount the story of one of their subjects who had entered an art history course in college as a subjectivist. The professor insisted that the discussion proceed beyond her subjective reactions to paintings to a more analytic discussion of form, color, style, and so on. The professor, in essence, forced her into a procedural way of thinking about objects as separate from herself. Their observation that certain types of pedagogical methods might promote procedural knowing is key to arguments developed in subsequent chapters of this book.

Constructed Knowing

Finally, the fifth orientation is constructed knowing, an orientation in which emotion and intuition are integrated with reason. It is distinguished by a view of knowledge as constructed, tentative, and contextual. Belenky et al. (1986) wrote that women with this orientation

> told us that their current way of knowing and viewing the world ... began as an effort to reclaim the self by attempting to *integrate* knowledge that they felt intuitively was personally im-

portant with knowledge they had learned from others. They told
of weaving together the strands of rational and emotive thought
and of integrating objective and subjective knowing. (p. 134)

Women who held this perspective had moved beyond subjective
knowing and procedural knowing to find a balance of the two because each alone had proved inadequate. Belenky et al. described
constructivist knowing as an extension of connected knowing, in
which individuals seek linkages between their own experience and
the phenomena they are attempting to understand. Perhaps most
significantly, constructivist women develop "a passion for learning" (p. 140). Because they understand themselves to be construc-
tors of knowledge, they enjoy the process of inquiry and are reflective about their own cognitive processes.

Women with this orientation also develop a new understanding of science and experts:

To see that all knowledge is a construction and that truth is a
matter of the context in which it is embedded is to greatly expand the possibilities of how to think about anything, even those
things we consider to be the most elementary and obvious. Theories become not truth but models for approximating experience. (p. 138)

Theorizing is not just "intellectualizing," as it is seen by those with
a subjectivist orientation, but a useful way of thinking about complex phenomena. The authors wrote that constructivist women are
not threatened by contradictions between experts and that they
have a high tolerance for ambiguity and complexity. They are challenged by problems of inquiry and can cut across disciplines and
perspectives to approach problems.

Another distinguishing feature of constructivists is their approach to moral dilemmas. First, perhaps because this position is
a type of connected knowing, these women had a heightened capacity for empathy and sensitivity to others (p. 143). Unlike received knowers who find moral truth in what authorities say, or
subjective knowers who rely on intuition as a source of truth, constructivists inquire about and reflect on the alternatives before
them and place at the center of those decisions the idea of caring
and "doing the best possible for everyone that is involved" (p. 149).
Belenky et al. noted that whereas women with other positions also

spoke about caring for others, constructivists tended to insist that holding an opinion entailed a commitment to action on behalf of others:

> Most constructivist women actively reflect on how their judgments, attitudes, and behavior coalesce into some internal experience of moral consistency. More than any other group, they are seriously preoccupied with the moral or spiritual dimension of their lives. Further, they strive to translate their moral commitments into action, both out of a conviction that "one must act" and out of a feeling of responsibility to the larger community in which they live (p. 150)

Belenky et al. found that these women in particular aspired to contribute to improving the quality of the lives of others. In the next chapter, this perspective and its emphasis on reflection, continuous learning, and synthesizing rational and emotive thought takes on new meaning in light of Dewey's discussion of the intellectual perspective that teacher educators ought to strive to cultivate in teacher candidates.

ANALYSIS OF THE STUDY

For the purposes of the argument forwarded in the following chapters, Belenky et al.'s (1986) model is relied upon, though tentatively, for a description of epistemological positions. It does improve greatly upon Perry's study in broadening the sample to include individuals of different social class backgrounds, ages, and ethnicities, and is therefore more generalizable, particularly to an examination of teacher candidates and teachers. Unfortunately, the issue of whether black women may have distinct ways of knowing is not addressed by Belenky and her co-authors, although other researchers have explored this question (Luttrell, 1989). Clearly, more research needs to be conducted on how the ways of knowing that Belenky et al. constructed from this data may relate to particular racial and ethnic groups' modes of interpreting the world.

In addition to their broadened sample, another strength of Belenky et al.'s work is their attempt to understand these cognitive processes as culturally bound. In contrast to Kohlberg (1981), for example, who asserted that moral development proceeds along a universal sequential path of stages that are structured wholes, these orientations to knowing cannot be separated from the cultural context that gives rise to them. If society were less patriarchical, for example, the position of silence might not be a part of this model. These orientations are perhaps best conceived as different solutions to the dilemma of integrating rational and emotive thought, some of which are more satisfactory than others, in a culture that socializes women (and men) in particular ways. In other words, Belenky and her co-authors' (1986) work provides insight into the psychological challenges to women's intellectual growth in this culture.

Criticisms

One of the most interesting criticisms of *Women's Ways of Knowing* is that the developmental model itself is prejudicial to women. Stone (1987) asserted that the finding that almost half of the sample of women in the study were predominantly subjectivists is troublesome. She asked, "Are we to conclude that almost half of all women are immature thinkers? Must not we then ask if a standard prejudicial to women is being applied to their ways of knowing?" (p. 309). One response to this issue is to recall that these "ways of knowing" are not exclusive to women, that they are also characteristic of men's thinking. This point is supported by Freidson (1970), who found a perspective nearly indistinguishable from subjective knowing in the clinicians he studied. Second, the test of whether this model is detrimental to women is not in the findings regarding the percentage of women who are subjectivists—to do so, in a sense, is to blame the messenger. On the contrary, whether or not this standard is detrimental to women depends on the consequences of the standard to women's continued intellectual growth and empowerment. To prize or esteem subjective knowing simply because a large proportion of women have that orientation would be socially reproductive in consequence—shifting the focus away from institutional and cultural barriers to women gaining a credible and powerful voice.

Stone (1987) is also concerned about the social class distribution of subjectivists. Belenky et al. (1986) reported that the subjectivists in the study tended to come from less advantaged and less achievement-oriented homes and tended not to be enrolled in the prestigious women's college that served as a site for the study, although some subjectivists did come from more advantaged backgrounds. Stone asked, "Now are we to believe that advantaged, white, well educated women are 'better' thinkers than their less advantaged counterparts . . . ?" (p. 309). The finding that subjective knowing is more common, although not exclusive, to less advantaged women is hardly surprising. Studies have shown that college preparatory and affluent schools tend to give emphasis to higher-order thinking skills, while schools populated by the working class focus on memorization of inert facts and socialization for working-class occupations (see for example, Anyon, 1981; Oakes, 1985). Again, these findings regarding the social class distribution among the ways of knowing signal the need to examine how schools themselves are detrimental to these students, rather than indicating that this model of intellectual growth is classist.

Differences Between the Findings of Perry and Belenky and Colleagues

This summary of the findings of Belenky and colleagues raises an important issue: How are these *women's* ways of knowing? What did Belenky et al. find by listening so carefully to women that Perry did not hear from men? Comparing and contrasting Belenky et al.'s findings with Perry's are difficult because Perry's findings conflate gender and class. For example, elite men's changing perception of authorities as a source of knowledge may not be purely a function of gender. It is therefore difficult to discern what is unique to men's versus women's ways of knowing, although some generalizations might be tentatively advanced.

One way to contrast Perry's findings with Belenky et al.'s lies in the discovery of the salience of psychological connection in the experience of the women in the latter study. Belenky and her coauthors pointed out that essential to women's growth is connection, that is, listening to others talk and developing the capacity to listen to the voice within themselves. In short, Belenky et al. found that generally women learn through empathy and communication, not through detachment. This emphasis on connection contrasts with Perry's emphasis on the importance of separation and abstraction for men's growth (see Lyons, 1990, p. 169):

> The tendency for women to ground their epistemological premises in metaphors suggesting speaking and listening is at odds with the visual metaphors (such as equating knowledge with illumination, knowing with seeing, and truth with light) that scientists and philosophers most often use to express their sense of mind. . . . Visual metaphors, such as "the mind's eye," suggest a

camera passively recording a static reality and promote the illu-
sion that disengagement and objectification are central to the
construction of knowledge. Visual metaphors encourage stand-
ing at a distance to get a proper view, removing—it is believed—
subject and object from a sphere of possible intercourse. Unlike
the eye, the ear requires closeness between subject and object.
(Belenky et al., 1986, p. 18)

Thus, metaphors such as voice and silence appear to more accu-
rately capture women's experience of intellectual growth than the
metaphors of vision.

There are other differences in the models as well. For example,
Perry did not find in his sample the position that Belenky et al.
call "silence." That finding is not surprising, given that women
who could be characterized in that way were often subjected to
physical or psychological abuse or both and had grown up in de-
meaning circumstances. Elite men are generally unlikely to have
grown up under those conditions. In addition, Perry does not
include in his model the position Belenky et al. describe as connected procedural knowing. Both studies found individuals in positions of dualistic/received knowing perspectives, in a subjec-
tivist/multiplicity orientation, and finally, in a relativistic/
constructed knowing orientation.

Of course, Belenky et al.'s (1986) psychological model of
women's intellectual growth cannot in itself provide aims of education. The aims that teacher education ought to seek with respect
to the intellectual perspectives of teacher candidates are the topic
of the philosophical inquiry of the next chapter. However, the construct of clinical consciousness coupled with Belenky et al.'s descriptions of women's ways of knowing provide insight into how
the specific intellectual perspective we might seek in teacher candidates may be cultivated. The discussion to follow will turn to
some of the issues that the research of Freidson and Belenky et al.
have raised for teacher education.

IMPLICATIONS FOR TEACHER EDUCATION

The precise stance teacher education should take toward clinical consciousness is the topic of the next chapter. It is important
to note here, however, that because nearly half of the women in
the *Women's Ways of Knowing* study could be classified as subjec-

tivist in orientation, not only may teachers be clinically minded as they work in school settings, but many teacher candidates may also be subjectively oriented as they enter teacher education. An unknown, but no doubt substantial number of candidates are also likely to have the received knowledge orientation, dependent on authorities for knowledge. It is reasonable to assert that the vast majority of teacher candidates are likely to manifest one or the other of these two perspectives.

This study suggests several hypotheses regarding teacher education. First, if Belenky et al.'s analysis is accurate, subjectivists will be intuitive, prize personal experience, and, on the basis of their firsthand experience, reject the texts and words of scholars. These candidates will claim that the best way to learn how to teach is through practica and field observations, with education courses having little perceived value for future practice. Indeed, some research bears out teacher candidates' preference for early and prolonged field work and devaluation of classroom study (Book, Byers, & Freeman, 1983).

Although Lortie (1975) suggested that teacher candidates may resist the lessons of professors of education because of their long apprenticeship of observation, Belenky et al.'s findings imply that many teacher candidates may do so because of their general epistemological orientation. Professors of education, particularly those in the social foundations of education, are likely to be seen as not sharing an experiential base with students. We could also expect that teaching through lecture would be extremely inefficacious with those who hold this perspective. For learners who claim to know through their firsthand experience, didactic methods are likely to be perceived as merely academic.

Belenky et al. (1986) wrote that subjective knowing is often challenged by professors in various disciplines. They suggested that some students are prodded into procedural knowing because they are forced to think in procedural ways. As mentioned before, one of the women in the study recalled being required to think procedurally in an art history class and this experience facilitated the transformation of her thinking. This observation leads one to ask whether clinical faculties, responsible for the pedagogical training of teachers, promote intellectual growth or reinforce clinical consciousness among their students. Much evidence suggests that teacher educators, those directly responsible for teaching methods courses and supervising practica and student teaching, tend not to engage in analysis, theoretical thinking, research, and abstraction as much as their colleagues in other disciplines (Lanier & Little, 1986). The consequences accruing to teacher educators who maintain a clinical consciousness in the university setting is explored further elsewhere (Raths, Katz, & McAninch, 1989). If professors themselves possess a clinical consciousness, it is highly likely that the clinical consciousness and subjectivist orientations that candidates bring into teacher education are reinforced, rather than challenged, in these departments. This could explain in part Lortie's (1975) finding, which has been supported by others (see, for example, Grant & Sleeter, 1986), that teaching is heavily biographical, as well as findings on the limited impact of preservice teacher education programs in general (Zeichner & Tabachnick, 1981).

A second hypothesis relates to individuals who both enter teacher education and graduate with the received-knowledge orientation. The observation that received knowers often shift to subjective knowing when faced with crisis and in the failure of male authority raises questions about the "sink or swim" phenomenon described by Lortie (1975). The "reality shock" of assuming the authoritative role of teacher, with only "primitive" inductive arrangements, has been described as the most profound kind of crisis for novice teachers. Isolated, often finding that what the college professor advocated does not seem to work in practice, the received knower is thrust into an ambiguous context that, it has been argued, promotes an intuitive and pragmatic perspective. For these reasons, it is highly possible that these individuals, too, would develop a clinical consciousness rather rapidly after assuming classroom responsibilities. The "sink or swim" experience, it would seem reasonable to assert, is precisely the kind of crisis that could prompt the shift from the received knowing to the subjectivist perspective.

Most significant, the analysis of the conditions of teaching also suggests the possibility that most teachers work in settings that never promote movement to a more "voiced" position, that is, procedural knowing or constructed knowing. But not all teachers' workplaces maintain norms of individualism and some do find organizational ways to minimize the ambiguity and pressures inherent in teaching. These schools, however, are in the minority (Rosenholtz, 1989). If the organizational conditions of most schools promote a clinical orientation, teachers as a group may not be able to progress to other epistemological positions: the context of teaching may actually arrest growth beyond clinical consciousness.

Finally, it is interesting to consider the possible outcomes for

procedural or constructed knowers who enter teacher education.
It might be that if they are pressed to be subjective knowers by
university clinical faculty, public school staff, and the organizational conditions of work, these candidates might find teaching
unsatisfying and leave the profession. Another possibility is that
they may compartmentalize their "ways of knowing," remaining
procedurists or constructivists in some domains, but assuming
a clinical perspective with respect to teaching. In other words,
it seems plausible that these ways of knowing may not be
worldviews that transcend context, but rather may be domain specific. This would enable, for example, the biology teacher, steeped
in scientific method, to be a procedural or constructivist knower
vis-à-vis his or her discipline, but maintain a clinical consciousness regarding teaching.

The idea that the ways of knowing may be domain specific,
rather than global worldviews, signifies an added dilemma for
teacher educators. The challenge may not only be to examine the
consequences of these ways of knowing for teaching practice and
the education of teacher candidates or to cultivate particular ways
of knowing, but also to help teacher candidates bring particular
ways of knowing to bear in domains in which, for one reason or
another, a specific perspective is regarded as irrelevant. Hargreaves (1984) reported a study that focused on teachers' collective
decision making regarding curriculum in an English middle
school. He found that although at the time of the deliberations
one teacher was taking a sociology of education course and was
familiar with a wide range of literature that critiqued current curricular practices, and two other teachers were married to lecturers
at the nearby college of education, references to educational theory or research were virtually absent from the discussions. Instead, teachers overwhelmingly cited their own classroom experience as the basis for forming curricular decisions. Hargreaves
(1984) wrote of this exclusion of educational theory from the discussions:

> When teachers are chained to the incessant routines and stric-
> tures of classroom life. . . . this is perhaps excusable. But when
> teachers. . . . become engaged in an educational activity whose
> central purpose is the reshaping of the whole curriculum in rela-
> tion to high-level aims concerning the contribution of school to
> society, we should perhaps worry that they do not consider or
> refer to what some of the most careful and detailed scholarship
> has produced in response to these very questions. (p. 248)

Hargreaves argued that evidence other than personal experience in the classroom was "culturally excluded" in these deliberations. For teacher educators, then, the issue is not just one of cultivating candidates' development in more sophisticated ways of knowing, but also their disposition to actually bring that thinking to bear on problems of practice. The perceived relevancy or irrelevancy of ways of knowing to specific domains invokes ideological issues that will be considered in the next chapter.

How can teacher educators themselves cope with the heterogeneity of their candidates' ways of knowing? One provocative means of attempting to educate teacher candidates who hold different perspectives toward knowing is suggested by Thies-Sprinthall and Sprinthall (1987). These theorists have forwarded a prescriptive model for teacher education based on descriptions of cognitive-developmental processes in several domains: conceptual development, based on the work of Hunt (1974); ego development, based on studies by Loevinger (1976); and moral development, based primarily on the work of Kohlberg (1981). Theis-Sprinthall and Sprinthall argued that these theoretical models of stage development provide a framework for teacher education programs.

Thies-Sprinthall and Sprinthall (1987) asserted that most teacher candidates, when assessed in these three domains, "are currently experiencing their world through one of two general modes" (p. 45). Interestingly enough, none of these three theories of adult development (Hunt, Loevinger, or Kohlberg) includes an orientation or stage resembling Belenky et al.'s subjective knowing or Perry's multiplicity. The modes Thies-Sprinthall and Sprinthall describe are labeled Mode A and Mode B. Mode A echoes received knowing, in which individuals view learning "from a concrete factual basis—there is one right way to teach" (p. 45). Mode A learners are also other directed and conform to social conventions. Mode B is characterized by an orientation toward "learning from an abstract perspective" and greater autonomy, and may include a capacity to distinguish between "social conventions and laws" (p. 45).

Thies-Sprinthall and Sprinthall (1987) advocated a tracking approach to accommodate developmental differences among teacher candidates. They suggested that the Mode A track curriculum include an emphasis on concrete tasks, close supervision by teacher educators, heavy use of advance organizers, and plenty of opportunities for guided practice. Track B students would be subjected to much less supervision and more opportunities for open-ended and theoretical projects. Thies-Sprinthall and Sprinthall insisted that this differentiation is aimed at matching "the learning tasks to individuals' current preferred learning style" (p. 48) and that Track A individuals, when they were developmentally ready, would shift tracks.

The use of developmental theories as a basis to sort, label, track, and provide differential learning opportunities is problematic in light of studies on tracking (Oakes, 1985). These studies suggest that greater gains in growth might be made if all students were exposed to a variety of thinking. Contrary to the approach advanced by Thies-Sprinthall and Sprinthall, it is much more desirable to develop curricula that foster growth in all students in a heterogeneous setting, regardless of the developmental differences among students.

CONCLUSION

In the last two chapters, Freidson's (1970) construct of clinical mentality has been explicated and applied to the educational arena. The context of teaching has been analyzed as one that promotes the elements of clinical consciousness. Further, research by Belenky et al. (1986) on the epistemological orientations of women suggests that the perspective Freidson described may have, in part, a developmental source. The implications of these works for a feminized profession such as teaching are far-reaching. That many teacher candidates may enter their programs resistant to theory, abstraction, and research and then go out to the schools to work in contexts that reinforce their subjective outlook signifies that individuals' transition to more powerful modes of knowing is at risk. In the next chapter, the consequences of clinical consciousness for the practice of teaching are explored.

3

A Critical Examination of Clinical Consciousness

It does not pay to tether one's thoughts to the post of use with too short a rope.
—John Dewey, *How We Think*, 1910/1985; p. 289

Clinical consciousness is a coping mechanism in that it enables the teacher to function with a degree of skill comprised of intuition, which allows the teacher to pick up on cues of boredom, misunderstanding, or disruption among students and to address problems that are ill defined; faith in his or her practice, which may facilitate the teacher's taking action and accrual of feelings of satisfaction from the job; and pragmatism, which enables the teacher to persist in dealing with complex problems. A clinical worldview may indeed allow teachers to cope with classroom tasks; however, there are good reasons to find fault with this perspective. The first part of this chapter will discuss several limitations of the clinical worldview. This analysis is not exhaustive, but rather is meant to demonstrate why clinical consciousness is not an optimal orientation for teachers to hold. The second portion of this chapter will consider the implications of these findings for teacher education.

LIMITATIONS TO CLINICAL CONSCIOUSNESS

The salient characteristics of clinical consciousness are its subjectivism and individualism. Teachers who are clinically minded are not only often physically and socially isolated from their peers, but they are intellectually secluded as well, relying on their firsthand experience and gut reactions in making professional judgments. In the discussion to follow, three weaknesses of clinical consciousness are elaborated: that it is prone to error, impedes teachers' learning, and obstructs critical inquiry into teaching.

High Risk of Error

A major weakness of clinical consciousness is that as teachers go about the task of learning how to teach from firsthand experience and as they develop interpretations of classroom life, they do so "empirically," as Dewey used the term (Dewey, 1904, 1910/1985, 1916, 1929a, 1929b). Although the word *empirical* usually means "derived from experience," Dewey used the concept to signify a particular perspective or interpretation of experience—one that consists of a relatively low level of reflection. For example, Dewey (1910/1985) wrote of the tendency to make inferences on the basis of past experience, without an understanding of the principles or relationships involved, as an example of empirical thinking:

> A says, "It will probably rain to-morrow." B asks, "Why do you think so?" and A replies, "Because the sky was lowering at sunset." When B asks, "What has that to do with it?" A responds, "I do not know, but it generally does rain after such a sunset." (p. 293)

In this exchange, Dewey suggested, person A manifests an empirical perspective because he does not know of a principle that would connect these two events nor is one sought. This inference is based on prior observations of the two phenomena, and person A does not push these observations further to inquire into their connection. In short, empirical inferences depend "simply upon repeated conjunction among facts" (p. 293), rather than an understanding of their relationship.

Dewey (1929b) also suggested that empirical thinking rests in large part on the "accidents" of the past. Perhaps a certain solution worked before with apparently good results, so it is used repeatedly. To the extent that teachers learn to teach by finding methods through trial and error that seem to "work," without further investigation into why or how the method appears to succeed, their practice has only an "empirical sanction."

One of the difficulties in interpreting classroom life in this way is that empirical thinking carries a high risk of error. In fact, some philosophers have argued that the correctness of an empirical inference is largely due to good luck:

> This approach is certainly not to be condemned out of hand;
> occasionally it yields remarkable results, and sometimes no
> other method is available at a moment when action is urgently
> required. No one will deny that a blind man with a gun can
> conceivably kill a duck on the wing (A. F. Griffin, 1942, p. 23).

Although the accuracy of an empirical inference depends to a
large extent on chance, an additional problem is that there is no
way to distinguish accurate inferences from incorrect ones:

> While many empirical conclusions are, roughly speaking, cor-
> rect; while they are exact enough to be of great help in practical
> life . . . the empirical method affords no way of discriminating
> between right and wrong conclusions. Hence it is responsible
> for a multitude of *false* beliefs. (Dewey, 1910/1985, p. 294)

One error characteristic of empirical thinking is the *post hoc, ergo
propter hoc* fallacy, the belief that because one thing follows another, it follows because of the first (Dewey, 1910/1985). Hence certain interventions or practices may be inferred to be efficacious
when in fact the intervention is not the cause of the observed
outcome.

Empirical thinking, no doubt, takes place in all types of settings. It is important to point out, however, that in the classroom
not only are clinically minded teachers basing their practice on
apparent results, but that these beliefs often go unchecked and un-
challenged. As Freidson (1970) observed, in an isolated setting, beliefs and practices tend to be self-validating. Because classroom
observations are at the same time used to generate and validate
beliefs, they appear to be confirmed:

> Once formulated or adopted, theories and beliefs tend to persist,
> despite an array of evidence that should invalidate or even re-
> verse them. When "testing" theories, the layperson seems to re-
> member primarily confirmatory evidence and to ignore poten-
> tially disconfirmatory evidence. (Nisbett & Ross, 1980, p. 10)

Thus one of the primary weaknesses of clinical consciousness is
that there is a high risk of error in a context in which there are
"no epistemological safeguards" or checks (see also Hamm, 1988,
p. 87; see Scriven, 1979) and in which there is little pressure to
correct (Huberman, 1983). The work of D. J. Clandinin (1985) pro-

vides an excellent example of a teacher's empiricism being implemented in practice.

An Example of Empirical Thinking in the Classroom.   Clandinin's (1985) effort to document and describe teachers' personal practical knowledge as images that are expressed in teaching provides an example
of empirical inference guiding teaching practice. The images
teachers use to guide practice, she found, are not derived from
teaching experience alone. Clandinin wrote of her research:

> My interest is in the imaginative processes by which meaningful
> and useful patterns are generated in practice. Propositional
> knowledge in this domain refers only to concepts of, and their
> relations to, practice. But practice involves more than this. It
> involves the calling forth of images from a history, from a narra-
> tive of experience, so that the "image" is then available to guide
> us in making sense of future situations. (p. 363)

Thus, Clandinin's "image" is a guide or template derived from
firsthand personal experience and expressed in the classroom.

Clandinin used participant observation and interviews to con-
duct her study of the personal practical knowledge held by two
Canadian school teachers, Stephanie and Aileen: the findings regarding the former will be related here. Stephanie, who teaches
in the early primary grades, has 12 years of teaching experience.

Clandinin found that Stephanie guided her teaching with a
"classroom as home" image. In short, she organized her classroom
around qualities associated with home: comfort, positive affect,
and cooperation. Clandinin wrote:

> In the interview Stephanie indicated the classroom was "a
> home." Her classroom was her "idea of how a home should be,"
> "a group of people interacting and cooperating together. . . ."
> She felt it "should feel comfortable there" and that "you have to
> have a feeling for the place because if not, I think it shows, it
> shows in your work, it shows in how you work with the children,
> it shows in the children themselves, how they relate to each
> other." (pp. 369–370)

How did this image translate into Stephanie's actions as a
teacher? Clandinin noted that Stephanie spent a great deal of
her own time and money on making the classroom attractive and
festive for holidays such as Halloween. In fact, Clandinin noted,

Stephanie came to school over the weekend to decorate the class-room for Halloween. She added that on one occasion Stephanie rejected Clandinin's offer to read a story to the class "in favor of making the room more home-like" (p. 374). Clandinin documented Stephanie's seemingly tireless efforts at creating a comfortable and festive environment for her students.

Several personal experiences, according to Clandinin, shaped Stephanie's image of the classroom as home. Stephanie reported that she always felt like an outsider throughout her formal educa-tion—including her years as a teacher candidate:

> She described her own school experiences as a "packaging" ex-perience and felt that those who did not fit the package were "scattered by the side" by the educational system. She describes herself as one of the ones who didn't fit the package and was "left out." (p. 372)

Clandinin attributed Stephanie's image to an effort to make the classroom a place where she and her students feel "at home." Clan-dinin wrote, "She spent then, as she continues to do now, long hours creating an environment in which she and her students could feel comfortable and cared for, in short, a home environ-ment" (p. 373).

An Analysis of Inferential Error. If Clandinin's interpretations are cor-rect, Stephanie used the "classroom as home" image to guide her teaching activities. The image evolved, Clandinin wrote, out of Stephanie's experience as a child and teacher candidate. Her prac-tice has only an empirical sanction because it is not based on any theoretical analysis or inquiry, nor does there seem to be any basis for her image other than the assertion that everyone in the class-room ought to feel comfortable.

No doubt there are good reasons why teachers, especially those in the primary grades, should expend much effort on creat-ing a homelike environment. Research bears out the significance of positive affect for student learning (Walberg, 1986), and many philosophers of education during the progressive era argued again and again for continuity between the home and school. Yet, in some respects, the classroom must be different from the home. The school is a special agency, set aside explicitly for the purpose of, among other things, formal learning.

It is interesting to note that Clandinin (1985) did not report any cognitive aims that Stephanie worked to meet over the course of the study or relate that Stephanie accrued satisfaction from student learning. Stephanie vetoed Clandinin's offer to read the children a story and asked her instead to help decorate the room. Stephanie's personal experience of feeling uncomfortable in school may legitimately provide a basis upon which to reflect on how to promote inclusion in her classroom, but simply as an outgrowth or accident of her own experience, the "classroom as home" image is held on weak grounds (see Buchmann, 1983). The role of teacher makes it incumbent upon members of the occupation to uphold certain commitments and responsibilities that supercede the accidents of their idiosyncratic biographies.

This discussion illustrates a major weakness of clinical consciousness and the empiricism that characterizes it: that it is prone to error and that it can proceed without challenge. Most recently, the pitfalls of this perspective have been illuminated by Buchmann and her colleagues (Buchmann & Schwille, 1983; Feiman-Nemser & Buchmann, 1985; Floden, Buchmann, & Schwille, 1987). It follows that to the extent that teachers are clinical in their outlook, researchers must use the terms *theory, knowledge*, and *wisdom* cautiously when describing teachers' understandings of their work.

Resistance to Learning

One quality of subjective knowing is a resistance to the expertise of others: the inner voice is the source of truth and it, rather than formal inquiry, is the mode for testing external sources of knowledge. One consequence of the subjectivism and individualism characteristic of clinical consciousness is that sources of knowledge other than firsthand experience are deemed uninformative to practice. Books, journal articles, and other secondhand knowledge, including the lessons of teacher educators, are devalued. Teacher candidates who possess a clinical consciousness as they enter teacher education are therefore likely to be uncoachable because they believe they have an "infallible gut" that tells them what is true. Teachers who are clinically minded are similarly immune to secondhand knowledge and therefore what they can learn about teaching from these other sources is severely constrained. Dewey (1904) wrote that learning to teach empirically means that

> The student adjusts his actual methods of teaching, not to the
> principles which he is acquiring, but to what he sees succeed
> and fail in an empirical way from moment to moment: to what
> he sees other teachers doing who are more experienced and suc-
> cessful in keeping order than he is; and to the injunctions and
> directions given him by others. (p. 14)

Dewey described a number of consequences associated with this
mode of learning to teach. First, teachers stop growing profession-
ally; they "seem to know how to teach, but they are not students
of teaching" (Dewey, 1904, p. 15). Their development as teachers is
confined to merely refining skills, and they are destined for "intellectual subserviency"(p. 16). Second, theory and practice fail
to join, resulting in what Dewey called "the unconscious du-
plicity, which is one of the chief evils of the teaching profession"
(p. 15).

As a consequence, techniques and methods that have been
challenged by research often survive long after they should have
been abandoned—and in the same way, new and promising findings described in journals or inservice programs have a weak or
delayed impact on practice (see Freidson, 1970). One example of
an obsolescent technique in teaching is ability grouping, which
has been condemned by researchers as having negative academic
and social consequences (Corno & Snow, 1986). Yet, the practice
persists. Some critics might go so far as to argue that in extreme
cases, a form of educational malpractice is the result of this *a
priori* devaluation of often better reasoning. It should be clear that
this is not a call for a research hegemony in teaching or mere
research knowledge use (see Buchmann, 1984); rather, it is a criticism of the maintenance of norms that deem formal inquiry irrelevant to teaching practice.

The idea that learning to teach is primarily a matter of experience, of using one's common sense and instinct, is, ironically, intellectually repressive. The prizing of the qualities associated with
clinical consciousness and the maintenance of norms that hold
that research and scholarship are irrelevant to practice (Hargreaves, 1984) deter teachers' intellectual transcendence of their
experience. As a form of resistance, clinical consciousness no
doubt supports teachers' actions and provides a sense of identity
distinct from that of the armchair scholar, but it is also self-
defeating. The idea that great teachers are born and not made and
that experience, rather than knowledge, is the *sine qua non* of the

occupation supports society's commonsensical views of the occupation.

In addition, learning from the school of "hard knocks" is difficult and draining: it is truly "learning the hard way." One can speculate not only about the opportunities lost because of teachers' reliance on firsthand experience, but also about the personal cost to teachers resulting in stress and burnout. Resistance to learning from other sources places a heavy burden for success or failure on the individual teacher. Lortie (1975) pointed out that in teaching, the burden of failure is personal, not collective (see also Freidson, 1970). Because teachers' conceptions of practice are subjective and largely individually constructed, it is difficult to attribute failure elsewhere:

> In fields where people perceive their knowledge (and their ignorance) as jointly shared, the individual burden is reduced. A person can take comfort from his compliance with normal expectations within the occupation; he can feel that he did everything possible within "the state of the art." ... Thus the individual can cope with unpleasant outcomes by sharing the weight of his failure and guilt; his inadequacy is part of the larger inadequacy of the field. Teachers derive little consolation from this source; an individualistic conception of practice exacerbates the burden of failure. (Lortie, 1975, p. 81)

Therefore, the teacher is burdened not only with having to learn to teach through his or her own experience, but also with having to take personal responsibility for failure in his or her classroom. It might be observed that there is a circularity about this problem. Teachers who are clinically minded have a particularistic, subjective orientation, which is the very thing that prevents the occupation as a whole from establishing a shared culture. Without these shared understandings, teachers must "sink or swim" on the basis of their own individualistic understandings of the classroom. In short, teachers' individualistic and subjective orientation to practice is costly to the occupation as a whole.

Avoidance of Critical Examination

Finally, as noted earlier, because of the induction and socialization arrangements characteristic of the occupation, teachers must independently construct ways of perceiving and interpreting classroom events. Teachers' perceptions and interpretations are likely to be shaped by strands of popular ideology, not only about the nature of schooling and teaching (although this is bound to be a large portion of it), but also regarding human nature, intelligence, social class, race, and so on. These notions are not constructed as the teacher enters the classroom, but absorbed from the culture at large over a lifetime and brought into the classroom. These prior theories then color, shape, and inform perceptions and beliefs in subtle and not so subtle ways (see Nisbett & Ross, 1980). For example, ability grouping, intelligence testing, and programs for the gifted reflect certain beliefs about the nature of intelligence. To clinically minded teachers, whose intuition and personal experience tells them what is true, these beliefs may well go unexamined because they so often seem commonsensical and are so basic to our culture that they appear to be natural and unchallengeable (see also Brown, 1969). Katz (1974) refers to this phenomenon as "excessive realism" (p. 59).

A good example of teachers' failure to transcend their own commonsensical beliefs about race, class, gender, and disability is offered by Grant and Sleeter (1986). In their ethnography of a multiethnic working-class junior high school, Grant and Sleeter found that the predominantly white middle-class teaching force rarely challenged the status quo, either individually or as a faculty:

> The teachers were probably quite comfortable functioning in the world as it is, with a few exceptions. . . . Although the teachers were friendly with the students and liked them, they did not seem dedicated to seeing that the students attain the best in life, to providing students with the knowledge and skills to change society so that it can benefit oppressed people more, or to continually refining their teaching skills. At least, they were not dedicated to these things enough to rearrange their own priorities in order to do something for their students beyond "business as usual." (p. 229)

In other words, teachers who take the status quo to be true and formulate beliefs on unreflected-upon stereotypes grounded in personal experience—in this case predominantly white and middle-class experience—cannot imagine possibilities for these working-class students other than working-class futures. To promote the aspirations of students who might strive for something other than working-class lives requires more than "business as usual," which for these teachers consisted of teaching remedial skills and being nice. The teachers did very little to empower students in a school system that did not serve them well.

In a follow-up inquiry, Grant and Sleeter (1988) went back to talk to the students they had originally interviewed, only to find that whatever aspirations the students had held in junior high school for something better than their parents' status had disappeared by the time the students were in high school. In a grim appraisal, Grant and Sleeter wrote:

> In spite of students' interest in further education, in spite of their good behavior in school, and in spite of the fact that the majority had normal learning ability, both the junior and senior high school faculty (with the exception of a very few individuals) accepted students' failure to empower themselves through education, and in so doing, ensured that they would fail. . . . After tenth grade two things happened: The students started raising serious questions about their futures . . . and the school pulled out of their lives as much as it could. . . . The school's main effort became equiping them to take a minimum wage job after graduation. The school staff may have viewed it as inevitable that these students would not continue schooling—interviews with the junior high teachers found strong acceptance of this belief—but there is no inevitability here; the school actively helped it to happen. (p. 38)

The teachers' inability or unwillingness to step outside of their own white middle-class experience, which they took to be true, worked to limit these students' aspirations and was therefore socially reproductive (see Apple, 1979).

Thus, it might be argued that clinical consciousness is in fact a type of *unconsciousness*—a naiveté with respect to the imperatives and mechanisms of political and economic institutions (see S. McAninch, 1991). Freire's (1985) definition of political illiteracy is relevant here. He wrote that a political illiterate is a person who "has a naive outlook on social reality, which for this one is a given, that is social reality is a *fait accompli* rather than something that's still in the making" (p. 103). For social critics like Freire and Kozol (1990), this kind of naiveté serves as an important means of psychological protection for the affluent and relatively affluent who would find inquiry into institutional mechanisms of status and privilege painful and threatening.

Miller (1977) referred to this type of psychological self-protection as a "convenient defect of vision." In his critical biography of Thomas Jefferson, Miller asserted that Jefferson, the brilliant political theorist, philosopher, architect, inventor, and revolutionary, failed to wield his considerable analytic powers in matters pertaining to slavery and race. Drawing on the work of Miller, S. McAninch (1991) wrote

> While Jefferson could by no means completely block out the evil of slavery, nevertheless the gaps in logic and application of scientific rules of evidence which allowed him to stereotype blacks as incapable of serious intellectual accomplishment and republican citizenship at least made the guilt and contradictions of being an enlightened man dependent upon slave labor manageable. (p. 3)

Jefferson's defect of vision, his lapses into forming judgments about slavery based on his personal experience with blacks and the pseudoscience of the eighteenth century, served his interests well. He, like the teachers in Grant and Sleeter's study, was unwilling or psychologically unable to critically inquire into matters of race.

Aside from protecting the status quo and their class position, teachers' maintenance of a clinical consciousness affords at least one more benefit. Teaching, as described in Chapter 1, is a demanding, complex practice for which its practitioners are underpaid and underappreciated. To maintain a clinical consciousness is to avoid the additional pressure to conceptualize a defensible philosophy of education—a philosophy that would necessarily entail a consideration of the social, moral, and political dimensions of teaching. In his classic study *Are American Teachers Free?*, Beale (1936) found that

> the vast majority of teachers have never done enough thinking to work out an explicit social philosophy. . . . The chief concern of many of the most vocal is higher pay. . . . The majority of teachers do not know what a controversial subject is. All too many have no desire to learn. (pp. 13–14)

To work out such a theory requires abstract as well as concrete thought and the capacity to generalize and draw connections, as opposed to a particularistic outlook. Beale argued that teachers themselves tend to come from educational institutions that do not facilitate abstract or theoretical thinking and that tend to support existing social arrangements:

> Their training has been only in acquiring facts and attitudes passed on to them by parents or teachers in order that they in turn may pass them on to a new generation with the greatest pedagogical efficiency or the least mental effort for student or teacher. (pp. 13–14)

For some individuals, it is likely that the maintenance of a clinical consciousness is a matter of not having the educational opportunities necessary to cultivate analytic thought. For others, as noted in Chapter 2, clinical consciousness may express an unwillingness to reflect critically in this domain; thus, doubt and inquiry are deemed irrelevant to practice. To borrow Kozol's (1990) metaphor, these individuals have successfully taken the scalpel to their own brain, choosing the self-protective safety of their defective vision over more critical modes of thought. In either case, the outcome is the same: the critical examination of teaching practice is obstructed.

In summary, three weaknesses of clinical consciousness have been discussed. It has been argued that the clinically minded run a high risk of inferential error, and their practice is compromised because they are resistant to learning from secondhand sources. This self-reliance, in turn, places a heavy burden on individual teachers. Further, they are likely to absorb and take into the classroom ideological tenets that are unlikely to be examined and reflected upon and thus teachers may inadvertently help to perpetuate society's inequalities. In the next section, the discussion will turn to the problems clinical consciousness poses for teacher education.

TEACHER EDUCATION AND THE CLINICAL WORLDVIEW

Teacher education must address at least three issues related to clinical consciousness. First, should the clinical worldview be cultivated and developed by teacher educators; that is, should candidates be encouraged to have this orientation? Second, if not, is there an alternative to this worldview? And, if so, how might that alternate perspective be promoted?

Should Clinical Consciousness Be Developed?

Some scholars have argued that if clinical consciousness is efficient for practice, then teacher educators ought to cultivate it and refrain from efforts designed to encourage theoretical thinking in prospective teachers. For example, this position is advanced by Yinger (1987), although he used the term "language of practice," rather than clinical consciousness, to describe the perspective of experienced teachers. Jackson (1968) also wondered about the efficacy of educating teachers to be more "rational":

> If teachers sought a more thorough understanding of their world, insisted on greater rationality in their actions, were completely open-minded in their consideration of pedagogical choices, and profound in their view of the human condition, they might well receive greater applause from intellectuals, but it is doubtful that they would perform with greater efficiency in the classroom. On the contrary, it is quite possible that such paragons of virtue, if they could be found to exist, would actually have a deuce of a time coping in any sustained way with a class of third graders or a play-yard full of nursery school tots. (p. 149)

It seems likely that individuals who are unable to think concretely or pragmatically, who could not pick up on cues of boredom or misunderstanding from students, who are so reflective that they could not act, would not be successful in the classroom. In short, to disparage clinical consciousness out of hand because it is "unscientific" is to overlook the demands placed on teachers in the classroom and to underestimate the value of teachers' intuitive understanding of students and classrooms.

On the other hand, as already pointed out, clinical consciousness has specific weaknesses that not only hinder the practice of individual teachers, but also work against the advancement of the occupation as a whole. Teachers who are seeking more power over policy making and curriculum literally do not have a credible voice if they are clinical in their worldview. Clearly, teaching on an empirical basis is not a sufficient foundation for practice. The question remains: is it possible to demand greater "rationality" on the part of teachers without compromising their capacity to meet the demands of teaching? Dewey (1904, 1929a) answered this question affirmatively, providing a compelling conception of the relationship of theory to practice in teaching.

Using Theory to Transform Teachers' Perspectives

In his classic 1904 essay, "The Relation of Theory to Practice in Education," and in *The Sources of a Science of Education* (1929a), Dewey described the orientation to teaching that he believed teachers must possess in order to be truly effective. Condemning the empirical perspective described above, Dewey (1904/1977) forwarded as an alternative "habits of work" that are characterized by inquiry. This conception rested on his view of the relationship of theory to practice in education.

Dewey maintained that the relationship of theory to practice is an indirect one because teaching cannot be "rule-governed," that is, the findings of inquiry cannot be rigidly applied to practice as rules:

> No conclusion of scientific research can be converted into an immediate rule of educational art. For there is no educational practice whatever which is not highly complex; that is to say, which does not contain many other conditions and factors than are included in the scientific finding (1929a, p. 19).

Teaching, he argued, can never be reduced to formulas or techniques; by its nature it demands personal judgment. In the words of James (1958), teaching requires that "happy tact and ingenuity to tell us what definite things to say and do when the pupil is before us" (p. 24).

Instead, Dewey (1929a) maintained that the results of scientific inquiry must find their way into teaching practice through the observations and judgments of teachers. Thus the relationship of theory to practice is a mediated one:

> Laws and facts, even when they are arrived at in genuinely scientific shape, do not yield *rules of practice*. Their value for educational practice—and *all* education is a mode of practice, intelligent or accidental and routine—is indirect; it consists in provision of *intellectual instrumentalities* to be used by the educator. (p. 28)

In other words, scientific results function "through the medium of an altered mental attitude" (p. 30). To illustrate this relationship, Dewey gave an example of a scientific finding regarding the differential rates of development of boys and girls:

> The teacher who really knows this fact will have his personal attitude changed. He will be on the alert to make certain observations which would otherwise escape him; he will be enabled to interpret some facts which would otherwise be confused and misunderstood. This knowledge and understanding render his practice more intelligent, more flexible and *better adapted to deal effectively with concrete phenomena of practice* [emphasis added]. (p. 20)

Conceived of in this way, he argued, science is not opposed to personal judgment, but rather the latter is augmented and empowered by the former. The results of inquiry help the teacher perceive the phenomena of practice in broader and more flexible ways. In short, the teacher is "emancipated from the need of following tradition and special precedents" (p. 21), that is, from empiricism.

Dewey (1904) argued that for habits of work to have a "scientific sanction," the teacher must observe and judge according to the principles of philosophy, psychology, and other fields related to education, using these principles critically and intelligently, and "applying the best that is available" (pp. 14–15). In order for these habits to develop, he wrote, teacher candidates must study the philosophy and psychology of education such that these theoretical principles operate as second nature in perception: "Only when such things have become incorporated in mental habit, have become part of the working tendencies of observation, insight, and reflection, will these principles work automatically, unconsciously, and hence promptly and effectively" (p. 15). Dewey seemed to suggest here that if theories are the instruments of teaching, then teachers must have such facility with them that they are used almost without effort.

A strong theoretical background also prepares teachers to continue to grow in their work as teachers, Dewey argued. For him, this meant not simply reading pedagogical literature or attending seminars, but possessing an "intellectual vitality." In *Democracy and Education* (1968), Dewey described attitudes that are valuable in teaching, and there he wrote that

> intellectual growth means constant expansion of horizons and consequent formation of new purposes and new responses. These are impossible without an active disposition to welcome points of view hitherto alien; an active desire to entertain considerations which modify existing purposes. (p. 175)

In short, Dewey did not simply call for a teaching force armed with the latest theory, but for teaching to be a learned profession, in which teachers possess the disposition and skill to continue to thoughtfully study their own practice throughout their career. He wrote, "Unless a teacher is such a student, he may continue to improve in the mechanics of school management, but he can not grow as a teacher, an inspirer and director of soul-life" (Dewey, 1904, p. 15). The intellectual quality Dewey saw as vital to teachers is this capacity for growth, for theory and practice to "grow together out of and into the teacher's personal experience" (p. 15).

To summarize, Dewey argued that the relationship between theory and practice is indirect, operating through the enlightenment and transformation of the teacher's judgment. Teachers, he argued, must learn to observe classrooms according to theoretical principles as a key to escaping empirical habits of work. He also maintained that a strong theoretical background prepares a teacher to be a lifelong student of teaching, a quality Dewey saw as vital to the professional teacher. In these essays, Dewey recognized the complexity and pressures of teaching practice. Theoretical principles, he argued, must operate almost automatically, incorporated into mental habit, if theory is going to find its way into practice.

Other philosophers have also made a persuasive case that theory's proper role in practice is to transform the perspectives of teachers. For example, Peters (1977) wrote that

> most of teaching involves a highly subtle moralized interrelationship between persons which cannot be reduced to a collection of techniques without debasing the relationships involved and making them less than personal. The effect of theory should therefore be long term—the gradual transformation of a person's view of children, of himself, and of the situation in which he is acting. (p. 163)

Peters went on to tell the anecdote of the visiting professor of education who, after an evening seminar on morals, asked students how the discussion might change the next morning's practice. Peters continued:

> They cooked up a few bright remarks to satisfy his sensitivities, but what they said to each other after he had gone was that if he had been through the course he would not have asked such a damn silly question! (pp. 163–164)

The point here is that theory does not translate overnight into changes in practice, but works indirectly and slowly through the development of the teacher's understandings. It is this transformation of perspectives that is constitutive of education (Peters, 1967).

A more recent version of this view was forwarded by Fenstermacher (1986, 1987), who maintained that research affects practice through the practical arguments held in the minds of teachers. In these works, Fenstermacher argued that the benefit of educational research for practice is not in the generation of whole programs or agendas, but in the improvement of the premises that form teachers' practical arguments.

But Dewey's argument is forceful because he addresses the problem of choosing between teaching as an expression of personal judgment and teaching as a "scientific" endeavor. Dewey insisted that the dichotomy is a false one: it is not a choice between personal experience and intuition or science, but a question of how the latter can inform and liberate the former. The personal and the scientific must work together, Dewey argued, or else the teacher will fall into the traps of empiricism, dependent on precedent and trial and error.

Developing Constructed Knowing Through Teacher Education

It is highly significant that the dispositions and orientation described by Dewey as essential to truly effective teaching largely correspond with Belenky et al.'s (1986) fifth epistemological position, which they call constructed knowing. In short, women with constructed knowing orientations are capable and disposed to maintain the intellectual perspective Dewey saw as fundamental to the teaching profession. With this orientation, as noted in the previous chapter, women are able to synthesize what they know personally with the knowledge of others—they can exercise intelligent judgment. Such women were described as reflective and possessing a deep intellectual curiosity. For these individuals, as in the perspective Dewey forwarded, theories are not truths, but useful ways of thinking about and interpreting concrete experience. Supporting Dewey's assertion that individuals who develop the scientific habits described above can prosper in the classroom, constructed knowers were found to have a high tolerance for ambiguity and complexity. The position of constructed knowing and Dewey's conception of scientific habits of thinking embrace a sensitivity and connection to context, the exercise of intelligence, and the prizing of inquiry.

Further, constructed knowers are capable of participating in moral deliberation and action—of central importance in a non-neutral realm such as education. These individuals inquire into alternatives and weigh consequences before coming to a conclusion. It is precisely this capacity and willingness to reflect and act that the teachers in Grant and Sleeter's study (1986, 1988) lacked. As Dewey (1916) persuasively argued, to begin to inquire into the connections between our actions and the consequences that flow from them is to begin to take responsibility for their consequences and to be able to act with what he called an "end in view" (p. 146), to make our actions intelligent. It is hypothesized that constructed knowers' ability to think abstractly and concretely, their comfort with doubt and complexity, signifies an ability to formulate normative conceptions of education that are fundamental to teaching conceived of as a moral endeavor (see, for example, Tom, 1984).

How might teacher educators promote candidates' ability and disposition to engage in this perspective? In order to cultivate the ability to engage in constructed knowing, the work by Belenky and her co-authors suggests that the route from the subjective orientation to constructed knowing is often indirect, through procedural knowing. In other words, for theory and practice to come together and transform judgment, individuals must first be able to expand their own experience and adopt other ways of looking. Thus, providing opportunities for teacher candidates to systematically engage in connected procedural knowing would seem to be key to the development of the type of thinking that, it has been argued, is desirable in the field of teaching.

Connected procedural knowing is crucial for a number of reasons. Belenky et al. (1986) pointed out that constructed knowing is an extension of connected knowing, as learners first expand their own experience through the process of empathy, then become capable of judgment and reflection. This emphasis on teacher candidates' ability to be empathetic and connected to students recalls the positive or functional aspects of clinical consciousness. Abstracted, disconnected teachers are likely to be too aloof from the exigencies of classroom life and the pedagogical needs of their students. Strengthening the ability to connect is especially important for men, who in our culture are socialized to be autonomous. Also, connected procedural knowing, as Belenky and her colleagues point out, capitalizes on subjective knowers' way of learning: it prizes experience, rather than repudiating it. Therefore, activities designed to engage subjective knowers in connected procedural knowing are likely to facilitate intellectual growth and stand in stark relief to lectures, which these learners are likely to dismiss as academic and removed from their way of knowing. Finally, connected procedural knowing lends itself to the kind of theoretical analysis posited to be productive in teaching, in which theoretical principles and concepts are internalized and transform individual perspectives. By taking on various theoretical perspectives, teacher candidates can learn other ways of looking at concrete phenomena.

This last point raises the issue of the centrality of theoretical understanding as a goal of teacher education. Theoretical understanding is essential to the promotion of constructed knowing, to the perspective Dewey called for in teaching. Thus, pedagogical attempts to cultivate this way of knowing must include instruction in theory as a vital component.

Although candidates may master an array of theoretical perspectives and have the ability to think procedurally or constructively, they still may not have the disposition to do so. Thus, aside from promoting connected procedural knowing and teaching theory, teacher educators need to help candidates develop the habit of engaging in this type of thinking in the educational domain. In other words, another instructional goal is to help candidates construct or reconstruct their views of theory and inquiry as relevant to their work.

Thus, this analysis suggests the following instructional goals for teacher education: the development of connected procedural knowing as a means to constructed knowing, the promotion of theoretical understanding, and the strengthening of the disposition to bring theoretical principles to practice. These goals provide a rationale for new approaches to teaching in teacher education programs and more specifically, to a form of case method. A description of how the study of cases may provide rich opportunities for teacher candidates to grow toward these goals is offered in Chapter 5. Before turning to a specific proposal for the use of the case method in teacher education, it is useful to examine the experience of several other occupations that have used cases systematically in professional education programs. A survey of case methods is the topic of the next chapter.

CONCLUSION

Clinical consciousness, it has been argued, is both adaptive and maladaptive. It has several specific weaknesses that greatly limit the capacity of individual teachers and the occupation as a whole to advance. Dewey's conception of the intellectual habits that are effective in teaching provides a compelling vision for teacher education. He maintained that theory has a fundamental role in transforming the personal judgment of teachers. The clinical consciousness he wanted teachers to possess is "scientific" in the sense that it is highly reflective and principled. The work by Belenky et al. (1986) suggests that a means for developing the intellectual outlook Dewey described, their "constructivist" perspective, is through the cultivation of connected procedural knowing. A case method may provide a means of fostering this particular orientation. It may also furnish a more effective way of teaching theory to teacher candidates than do didactic methods. Furthermore, a case method that provides candidates with practice in bringing principles to bear on cases may strengthen the disposition to see theory as relevant to practice.

4

The Case Methods of Law, Medicine, and Business

Medicine and surgery must be learned, partly, it is true, from books, but largely from the bodies of the sick and wounded; whereas law is to be learned almost exclusively from the books in which its principles and precedents are recorded, digested, and explained. . . . The law library, and not the court or law office, is the real analogue of the hospital.
     —Charles Eliot, as cited in Chase, 1979, pp. 341–342

Dewey (1904) pointed out nearly 90 years ago that teacher education is a case of the more general task of educating individuals for the professions. At the time that Dewey wrote that essay, elite schools of law and medicine had already undergone their renaissance. These schools were distinguished from their less prestigious counterparts by many factors: selective admissions requirements, extended programs, full-time faculties, and perhaps most significant, a new curriculum that rejected a dependence on both didactic instruction and apprenticeship arrangements in favor of the scientific case method.

    In attempting to develop a case method or methods for their own field, teacher educators have examined how cases are used in the preparation of other professionals, particularly in the fields of law, business, and medicine (Carter & Unklesbay, 1989; Kleinfeld, 1992; Kowalski, Weaver, & Henson, 1990; Merseth, 1991a). Kowalski, Weaver, and Henson (1990), for example, asserted the efficacy of the case method in other professional curricula, such as law and business, and the utility of this approach in the preparation of teachers who, like executives and lawyers, are decision makers in a complex arena. Carter and Unklesbay (1989) concluded, based on their study of the legal case method, that the "resources necessary to produce, collect and catalogue teaching cases on a large scale simply do not exist" (p. 534). In her thoughtful analysis,

Merseth (1991a) found the business case method to be the most likely precedent for teacher education because of the similarities she saw between the kinds of knowledge needed for teaching and for working in the business world. It is unclear, however, given the analyses in Chapters 2 and 3, how readily a form of pedagogy developed for the graduate education of elite men can serve as a model for teacher education. The special challenges of promoting intellectual growth among primarily non-elite undergraduates, the majority of whom are women, have yet to be criteria for examining case methods in other fields.

In this chapter, the case methods of law, medicine, and business will be briefly examined with a primary focus on the theory of case teaching in each of these fields, in light of the analysis presented in previous chapters. The following questions will frame my discussion:

1. What are the instructional goals of the case method in each field?
2. Is it likely to foster the intellectual growth of women?
3. How are the cases in each field related to theoretical study?
4. What conception of practitioner thinking does each method embrace? Or, in other words, which way of knowing does each case method advance?

These issues are fundamental to an analysis that will assist teacher educators in the development of a case method that is more than a mere technique and that will best serve the special pedagogical demands of their field.

THE CASE METHOD IN LEGAL EDUCATION

When Charles Eliot selected Christopher Columbus Langdell to head Harvard Law School in 1870, pressures had already mounted for reforming legal education. The instructional goals of the legal case method cannot be understood apart from the factors that contributed to the invention of the case method and the eventual rejection of traditional methods of teaching the law; namely, lecture and recitation from traditional texts.

First, as social science disciplines vied for a place in higher education in the mid- to late nineteenth century, the law sought legitimacy as an appropriate field of study at the university. One means of achieving this legitimacy was to claim a scientific basis for the discipline and, indeed, Eliot and Langdell pushed the notion that the law is a science whose complexity justified university study. The scientific study of the law required new pedagogical methods and provided the impetus for the application of inductive methods to the field (Redlich, 1914).

Aside from the quest for status, a second important factor in the reform of the law curriculum was the burgeoning nature of the legal literature itself. The growth of the courts at all levels and the passage of laws at the municipal, state, and federal levels had produced a general state of organizational chaos from the point of view of the profession during the nineteenth century. When Langdell assumed his position at Harvard Law School, there were nearly 2,000 volumes of American law reports; the need for systematization—at least for pedagogical purposes—was dire (Reed, 1921).

Finally, the university law school had to compete with the most prominent mode of preparation for the bar: the apprenticeship. Even at the turn of the century, most lawyers studied for the bar through some form of law office internship. The law curriculum had to prove its efficacy and superiority to these less formal methods of legal study (Redlich, 1914).

Langdell's Instructional Goals

These three pressures—to advance the claim that the law is a scientific field of study, to accommodate the growth in the legal literature, and to institutionalize and formalize legal education—were all addressed by Langdell's version of the case method. The law curriculum under Langdell reflected his devotion to the idea that the law is a science and its data are adjudged cases:

> *Law, considered as a science, consists of certain principles or doctrines. To have such a mastery of these as to be able to apply them with constant facility and certainty to the ever-tangled skein of human affairs, is what constitutes a true lawyer; and hence to acquire that mastery should be the business of every earnest student of law.* Each of these doctrines has arrived at its present state by slow degrees; in other words, it is a growth, extending in many cases through centuries. This growth is to be traced in the main through a series of cases. (as cited in Redlich, 1914, p. 11)

Langdell viewed legal doctrine as simply another species of truth that could be discovered and mastered through scientific methods. Unlike his predecessors, however, Langdell placed these data (the cases) in the hands of his students and insisted that the curriculum could consist entirely of case study. From cases, principles would be induced and the evolution of true legal doctrine traced (see Gilmore, 1977).

From a pedagogical standpoint, this approach provided one solution to the problem of the burgeoning legal literature because only those cases that contributed to doctrine needed to be included in the course of study. Langdell's casebooks of chronologically arranged appellate court cases, devoid of commentaries, treatises, or supporting materials, forwarded the idea that the law is self-contained and evolving in the text of the cases (Friedman, 1973).

Finally, Langdell combined case study with Socratic teaching. The case method as Langdell practiced it required active participation on the part of the student, as opposed to earlier methods that simply required memorization of textbooks or lectures.

> Under the old method law is taught to the hearer dogmatically as a compendium of logically connected principles and norms, imparted ready made as a unified body of established rules. Under Langdell's method these rules are derived, step by step, by the students themselves by a purely analytical process out of the original material of the common law, out of the cases (Redlich, 1914, p. 13).

Langdell's new instructional method replaced textbooks and lectures with Socratic discussion of appellate court cases that the students read firsthand. Most important, the case method was promoted as scientific in its approach, as students analyzed and induced legal principles from the cases.

Although Langdell is often credited with originating or inventing the case method, in his time inducing principles from objects was by no means a novel idea. Indeed, Pestalozzi's disciples in the United States had widely popularized the "object lesson." Eliot (1924), in his account of Langdell's years as dean of Harvard Law School, doubted that Langdell had any familiarity with the educational theories of Froebel or Pestalozzi. "Yet his method was a direct application to intelligent and well-trained adults of some of their methods for children and defectives" (p. 53).

Change of Emphasis After Langdell

Langdell's successors shifted the rationale of the case method to accommodate more complex theories of the law in the years after 1900. Under Harvard's Dean James Barr Ames and Harvard-trained Dean William Keener of Columbia, the development of legal reasoning became the primary rationale for the case method. As Stevens (1983) wrote, "Methodology rather than substance became the nub of the system" (p. 56). Ames's casebooks, reflecting this new emphasis, contained cases organized by topics rather than chronologically.

Describing in more detail what it means to "think like a lawyer," Keener wrote:

> The student is required to analyze each case, discriminating between the relevant and the irrelevant, between the actual and possible ground of decision. And having thus discussed a case, he is prepared and required to deal with it in its relation to other cases. . . . *By this method the student's reasoning powers are constantly developed*, and while he is gaining the power of legal analysis and synthesis, he is also gaining the other object of legal education, namely, knowledge of what the law actually is. (as cited in Redlich, 1914, p. 24)

Eliot, Keener, and others argued that the learning that accrues from students' independent construction of legal principles through the study of cases is more lasting and powerful than the learning that results from the law professor pronouncing legal doctrine or from the legal apprenticeship.

To this day, case method and "thinking like a lawyer" are current in American legal education (see, for example, Scully, 1983). Although casebooks have been broadened to include supplementary materials, various clinical arrangements developed, and innovative curricula designed, the analysis of cases remains the cornerstone of education for the law (Stevens, 1970). It is important to note that claims about the efficacy of this method have historically been made without the support of research (Teich, 1986). Often, the evidence marshalled in favor of the case method was anecdotal in nature regarding the graduates of Yale and Harvard versus the graduates of some other non-case-method school.

Criticisms of the Legal Case Method

Criticisms of the case method, although at times made by powerful individuals within the legal community, appear never to have posed a serious threat to the Harvard model (Stevens, 1983). Yet, over the last century, several important issues surrounding the case method have been raised, and some of these are discussed below.

The case method has been argued by many to be a slow and inefficient means of teaching the law. Dean William Minor Lile of the University of Virginia Law School wrote in 1921:

> The most serious objection is the slowness with which the course goes forward, and the gaps that the method must leave in the continuity and completeness of the topics pursued. If the student had six years to devote to his law school course, instead of three, the case method might prove ideal. (as cited in Stevens, 1983, p. 192)

The slowness of the case method has prompted some scholars to wonder if three years of case study was too much (see Stevens, 1983).

During the period when legal formalism was on the wane and legal realism was emerging after World War I, the basis for the case method—the law as science premise—came under sharp attack. In fact, Stevens (1983) suggested that "there was a legitimate revulsion against many aspects of Langdell's case method of teaching," especially the notion that the law was objective (p. 141). Legal realists such as Jerome Frank and Karl Llewellyn maintained that the legal establishment since the Civil War had been out of touch with the realities of society at large and that the law must respond to social change. Rejecting the adherence to precedent that had been the cornerstone of Langdell's case method, they emphasized the social policy aspects of the law. Thus, in this period, attempts were made to make the case method more problem oriented. The problem method, Stevens (1983) asserted, was not more widely adopted because it required special resources, including appropriate texts. Other schools attempted to use problem cases, which "omitted either facts, or the opinion or the decision, referring the student elsewhere for the omitted materials" (p. 215). Apparently, such approaches met some resistance from students who found the open-ended nature of the problems unsatisfying.

More recently, the case method has been attacked on several grounds. Some critics have asserted that the case method cultivates a narrow capacity to analyze cases and to construct forceful arguments on either side of a dispute at the expense of fostering a concern for the consequences of the outcome. Nader (1978) wrote of Harvard Law School:

> You do not go there to engage in a pervasive study of justice. Nor do you go there to learn how to comfort the afflicted and afflict the comfortable. The consensus of most law professors is that you go there to encounter and master the techniques of legal reasoning (p. xiii).

Nader joins other critics who assert that the Harvard model breeds "analytic giants but moral pygmies" (see Stevens, 1983, p. 121), individuals technically proficient, yet detached from questions of value and context.

The Legal Case Method and Teacher Education

This brief account of the case method in law indicates that this model of the case method would facilitate some of the instructional goals posited at the conclusion of Chapter 3, but deter others. The goals forwarded there included the promotion of connected procedural knowing as a means of developing constructivist knowing, the cultivation of theoretical understanding, and the strengthening of the disposition to bring principles to bear on practice.

Clearly, one of the virtues of this case method in light of these objectives is the manner in which the analysis of cases is related to the acquisition of theoretical understanding. As students are taught to trace lines of legal precedent through the study of cases, they acquire an understanding of legal principles. Even after Langdell's time, when the emphasis of the legal curriculum shifted to teaching legal reasoning, the idea of promoting students' understanding of legal theory continued to be embraced. The tightness of fit between case analysis and the acquisition of theoretical understanding is an advantage of the case method: the study of theory and of cases go hand-in-hand.

However, there are also two major disadvantages of the case method as it is applied to fostering women's intellectual growth. First, the type of knowing promoted through this method is separate procedural knowing. To think like a lawyer is to reason objectively through strands of legal precedent. Separate procedural knowing makes what is personal irrelevant and is therefore at odds with subjective knowing. From a pedagogical viewpoint, the cultivation of separate procedural knowing fails to build upon subjective knowers' view that firsthand experience is the most reliable source of knowledge. Connected procedural knowing, as pointed out in the last chapter, capitalizes on subjective knowers' orientation to learning because it does not reject the personal—it expands the learner's perspective to include the experience of others.

The cultivation of separate procedural knowing for the field of teaching is problematic for another reason as well. In teaching, there is no objective process that can be applied to problems of practice that will by definition produce a wise decision. As asserted in the previous chapter, teaching cannot be rule (or procedure) governed; thus the cultivation of this way of knowing is not appropriate for the field of teaching. Central to teaching are processes of connection, such as empathy, not of separation and objectification.

Further, if Nader (1978) is correct in his assessment that this case method promotes a dispassionate capacity to develop legal arguments on any side of an issue, then this is a type of thinking that teaching can ill afford. Because teaching is foremost a moral endeavor, educators cannot be neutral. The dispassion and disinterest of separate procedural knowing is inappropriate to this domain. Some critics have argued that the field of law itself maintains a masculine bias and that this type of reasoning is not appropriate for that field either (see Bartlett, 1990).

Finally, as a form of pedagogy, Socratic discussion is a kind of teaching that is particularly unlikely to promote women's epistemological growth. Because its aim is to question, challenge, and doubt, this kind of teaching may be threatening to women who are just beginning to develop their own sense of self and voice. Socratic discussion is the exact opposite of the kind of teaching that Belenky et al. (1986) see as key to women's growth because the teacher is the authority who sits in judgment of what the student claims to know. To make matters worse for women who are intimidated by this process, the professor's judgments are public. Further, the emphasis on independent construction of legal principles in the case method curriculum places autonomy and individualism at a premium, rather than the more feminine values of cooperation, connection, and care.

In sum, the greatest virtue of the legal case method is that the study of cases and theory proceed hand-in-hand, but it promotes a type of thinking that does not lend itself to the field of teaching and that fails to capitalize on subjective knowers' way of learning. Socratic teaching, which sets up the professor as an authority who doubts and tests what students say, is also unlikely to facilitate women's epistemological growth. In the next section, the medical case method is examined.

THE CASE METHOD IN MEDICAL EDUCATION

Modern medical education is generally divided into two periods: the preclinical and the clinical. In contrast to the law school curriculum in which cases are generally studied throughout the 3-year program, the systematic study of cases in medical education is usually reserved for the 3rd and 4th years of training. In this literature, the "case method" has referred to two different exercises: the clinical clerkship, in which medical students are formally assigned patients for diagnosis and treatment under supervision; and the "clinico-pathological conference," in which pathologists, interns, residents, and medical students study the medical records of a deceased patient. This discussion will focus on the clinical clerkship, the key clinical component of medical education.

The story of reform in medical education is, like that of the modernization of the law school, one of elite universities attempting to make graduate study more exclusive and scientific in the period following the Civil War. Again, Charles Eliot played a large role in advancing the medical school at Harvard. Of all the changes he implemented there, perhaps the most significant was the introduction of laboratory work in chemistry and other subjects (Beecher & Altschule, 1977). Although advances were made in leading universities in transforming instruction in the basic sciences, progress in teaching the clinical sciences lagged behind. Most clinical subjects continued to be taught through passive methods, such as lecture or amphitheater demonstrations or combinations of both. In fact, it was common for medical students in the nineteenth century to graduate without much personal contact with patients at all, although there were notable exceptions (Atwater, 1980).

The Clinical Clerkship

The transformation of clinical education into a scientific enterprise is often credited to Johns Hopkins Medical School and to Professor William Osler in particular. Not long after Johns Hopkins Medical School opened in 1893, it set the standard against which other medical schools were judged:

> Johns Hopkins was a radical departure in medical education. . . . Two years of instruction were provided in the basic sciences, with extensive laboratory work mandatory for every student, and two years of rigorous training were also provided in the clinical subjects, with the students gaining experience at the hospital bedside. (Ludmerer, 1985, p. 57)

Built with a $7 million bequest for both a medical school and an affiliated teaching hospital, Johns Hopkins afforded a rich opportunity for clinical teaching. Abraham Flexner, in his 1910 report to the Carnegie Commission, embraced the Johns Hopkins model and its emphasis on research (Thorne, 1973).

Soon after the medical school opened, Osler, a clinician dedicated to research, introduced the clinical clerkship on the wards of the Johns Hopkins hospital. The clerkship required students to take responsibility for five or more patients at a time under supervision. Medical students performed examinations, carried out medical procedures as necessary, diagnosed, and followed the patient's progress until the patient was discharged or died. Osler (1969) wrote, "In what may be called the natural method of teaching the student begins with the patient, continues with the patient, and ends his studies with the patient, using books and lectures as tools, as means to an end" (p. 180). Osler visited the wards several times a week to hear case histories, examine patients, and interrogate the medical student on his findings (Rothstein, 1987).

The clerkship embraced the new emphasis in medical education on firsthand scientific investigation (see Starr, 1982). In fact, Osler (1969) maintained that the training of the senses is a major task of clinical education:

> Teach him how to observe, give him plenty of facts to observe and the lessons will come out of the facts themselves. . . . The whole art of medicine is in observation, as the old motto goes, but to educate the eye to see, the ear to hear and the finger to feel takes time, and to make a beginning, to start a man on the right path, is all that we can do. (p. 180)

Thus, Osler sought a refined empiricism in his students, although he was far from denigrating scientific research or texts. Osler (1901) saw texts as essential components of medical study.

Generally, through this century, clerkships have been composed of a number of elements. The ward round provided an opportunity for the medical student to present his case to the supervising physician/professor and the other clerks in his group:

> The ward round held daily is both a teaching exercise and a professional call by physician on patient. Gathered about a bedside the group must first put the patient at ease. . . . The clerk then relates the history and his examination, and the occasion then becomes one of keen scientific observation and inquiry. (Means, 1948, p. 119)

Generally, the clerk is expected to present the patient's case history, suggest a tentative diagnosis, and defend his assessment to his professor.

Several factors were integral to the successful introduction of the clerkship at Johns Hopkins (Atwater, 1980, p. 167). Perhaps the most important of these was faculty control over Johns Hopkins Hospital. Without a university teaching hospital, clinical instruction could be offered only at the discretion and good will of hospital boards. The lack of satisfactory facilities for teaching clinical medicine at most universities and proprietary schools was cited by Flexner in his 1910 report as a major impediment to progress in clinical teaching (Atwater, 1980).

Changes in the Clerkship in This Century.   The clerkship has remained a mainstay of clinical medical education, although it varies from medical school to medical school (Rothstein, 1987) and has changed somewhat in this century (see Konner, 1987). Most of these changes have occurred because of the advances in medical sciences that have transformed medicine into a highly specialized, technical, and procedure-oriented practice (Atwater, 1980). Modern teaching hospitals "became sophisticated laboratories rather than infirmaries with nurses, as the hospitals of the nineteenth and early twentieth centuries had been. Technicians instead of physicians and students increasingly filled diagnostic and therapeutic functions" (p. 171). This transition limits medical student–patient contact because much of the diagnostic work is conducted away from the patient's bed by other people (Atwater, 1980; Rothstein, 1987).

Atwater also suggested that the growing use of patients at public hospitals for teaching means that medical students are often seeing patients who are sicker, but whose hospital stay is usually shorter, than was the case in the past. As a result of this shift in patient population, "the student often had a briefer and more superficial relationship with the patient, had less personal responsibility for him, and had less opportunity to perfect his own abilities" (Atwater, 1980, p. 171).

Criticisms of the Clerkship. Like the case method in law, the clerkship has been criticized on various grounds. One criticism of clerkships is that they provide a rather haphazard means of clinical instruction. Rothstein (1987) pointed out, "A sufficient number of patients with a particular disease were rarely available when the instructor wished to use them" (p. 109). On the other hand, clerks often had to study independently to care for patients in addition to performing all their other duties (Rothstein, 1987). The haphazardness of the distribution of disease on the wards, in other words, presented an additional burden to clerks.

Another issue pertains to the representativeness of the patients a medical student sees during the clerkship. Some critics have suggested that hospital patients are more ill and less affluent than most of the cases a doctor is likely to encounter in actual practice (Thorne, 1973). Others have asserted that extensive work with the chronically ill fails to teach students how to care for the less spectacular case, the ones physicians encounter most often in their own practice (Rothstein, 1987).

Another criticism relates to the growing instructional role played by the house staff (Rothstein, 1987). The teaching burden placed on them is disturbing because "studies have found that residents provided lower quality teaching than faculty members and attending physicians and that they considered their teaching responsibilities to be less important than their own education and their patient-care responsibilities" (p. 304). On the other hand, this is not to suggest that faculty members regard teaching as their first priority and are all excellent pedagogues; on the contrary, some evidence suggests that the quality of interaction between students and faculty members is generally quite poor (Foley, Smilansky, & Yonke, 1979; Rothstein, 1987).

In short, the quality of instruction provided during the clerkship is suspect. As the house staff assumes more and more of the teaching responsibilities and place themselves between the undergraduates and the medical faculty, faculty-undergraduate contact is undercut. New diagnostic technologies have also diminished the role of the undergraduate in the bedside care of the patient. Finally, it is unclear that the undergraduate clinical curriculum provides experience with cases that are representative of the types of cases that constitute the vast majority of medical practices.

The Case Method in Medicine and Teacher Education

Clinical medical education as it is described here involves training the physician in the analysis of signs and symptoms and the procedural application of rules and procedures derived from research to particular problems of practice. This model of case method promotes a kind of separate procedural knowing, although it differs somewhat from the type cultivated by the legal case method. During the clerkship, the physician's senses are honed for their value in diagnosis. As noted above, Osler sought the cultivation of the physician's powers of observation in the treatment of patients. This training in observation and sensing is, in fact, promoting a type of subjective knowing. The physician learns how to collect data through firsthand observation that in turn serves the larger process of applying rules and procedures to individual cases. Although the senses and firsthand experience are prized, this case method still promotes separate procedural knowing.

Not only does this case method forward separate procedural knowing, it lacks the virtue of maintaining the tightness of fit between theoretical study and case study that characterizes the legal case method. Here theoretical study and the analysis of cases do not proceed concurrently; there is therefore more of a haphazard quality to this case method. The mismatch between theory and cases and the unrepresentativeness of the sample of cases available for study is a major disadvantage of this method. As will be argued in the next chapter, theoretical understanding requires knowledge of cases that exemplify the specific theoretical class under discussion. For this reason, the chance convergence of theory and cases is a detriment to the aim of developing theoretical understanding. This concern is similar to those raised in teacher education regarding the narrowness of student teachers' clinical experience, which usually takes place in a single classroom (see Shulman, 1984).

This method also has a major pedagogical disadvantage from the standpoint of promoting women's development. As in the legal case method model, the instructor's role here is as doubter and tester, rather than facilitator and believer. Again, this is unlikely to promote the intellectual growth of women who are struggling to develop their own voice. In the next section, a third model of the case method will be examined: the case method in the field of business.

THE CASE METHOD IN BUSINESS EDUCATION

The literature on the case method as it is practiced in business schools suggests that there is no one "business case method." Cases are used in a variety of ways, ranging from constituting the core of a course to simply providing illustrative material for lectures. In addition, cases vary in form and content. Generally, a case in this field refers to a written account of a problematic situation confronting a firm that demands action on the part of an executive or group of executives.

This examination of the case method in the field of business will depart somewhat from the format of the previous discussion. Because cases are not generated by the practice, as they are in law and medicine, the focus here will be on the writing of the cases. The discussion will consider the development of the use of cases at Harvard Business School, the rationale for their use, the form and content of the cases, how they are used pedagogically, and finally, an evaluation of the method.

The Case Method at Harvard Business School

In 1908, the newly established Harvard Business School offered its first case class in the field of commercial law, using cases from the law school (Copeland, 1954). Because of the dearth of case material in other business areas, faculty members use a vari-

ety of artifacts to stimulate discussions, including business documents, reports, or a business problem:

> Instructors preferred the latter for they intuitively saw these
> problems as a bridge between academia and business. Business-
> men had to deal with a daily succession of problems (cases).
> Why not bring those problems to the classroom for apprentice
> managers' use? ("Teaching with Cases," 1987, p. 25)

In 1920, the Harvard Business School devoted research money
specifically to the purpose of case development. It hired a group
of its graduates to go out into the field to collect and write up
business problems. According to Smith (1987), "This guaranteed
both the growth of case material as we know it, and Harvard's role
as its main exponent since this date" (p. 53).

The Bureau of Business Research, which was active at Harvard from 1920–1925, accumulated business cases that were to
serve as precedents, although this idea was later criticized and
abandoned (Towl, 1969). After 1925, with the dismantling of the
Bureau, faculty members assumed responsibility for case research
and development.

Pedagogical Rationale for the Use of Cases in Business

Many of the early academics in the business school, as in the
law and medical school, wrote of the inadequacies of passive
methods of instruction for the purpose of meeting the primary
aims of the school; that is, the training of executive judgment.
From the early days of Harvard Business School, the case method
was forwarded as a means of improving decision-making ability
through the development of analytical skills. In 1951, a professor
at the business school wrote that "the heart of the method is the
use of problems to train the student to discover and then to fix in
his mind *ways of thinking that are productive in the chosen field*"
(Hunt, 1951, p. 175). The objectives of developing problem solving,
decision making, and other process goals continue to be widely
cited as the primary aims of case method instruction (Schnelle,
1967; Smith, 1987).

Unlike the case methods in law or medicine, the emphasis in
business is on using the case method to stimulate thinking
through group discussion and analysis: "The case method is a type
of the discussion method of teaching, in which students partici-

pate in group analysis of a problem, thus being trained to think by the interaction of individual attempts to reach a decision" (Hunt, 1951, p. 176). Hunt also argued that group study of alternative solutions to specific business problems is more likely to promote the capacity to think than studying broad generalizations without cases.

Form and Content of a Business Case

Cases in business range from short descriptions of relatively simple business problems to highly complex narratives that include "internal company information as well as external industry data, and psychological, sociological, and anthropological observations as well as technical and economic material" ("Teaching with Cases," 1987, p. 26). Most of the literature on the business case, however, focuses on the "issue" or "classic" case.

Traditionally, a case is a record of a real-life problem confronting a manager or group of managers. For example, Lawrence wrote:

> A good case is the vehicle by which a chunk of reality is brought into the classroom to be worked over by the class and the instructor. A good case keeps the class discussion grounded upon some of the stubborn facts that must be faced in real life situations. . . . It is the record of complex situations that must be literally pulled apart and put together again for the expression of attitudes or ways of thinking brought into the classroom. (as cited in "Teaching with Cases," 1987, p. 26)

Thus, one of the elements of a business case is that it is based on the experience of a real firm and analogous to the type of problem future executives are likely to confront in their business experience.

The classic business case, aimed specifically at promoting decision-making skills, is open-ended in order to provide an opportunity for discussion and problem solving. For this purpose, more than one credible solution to the business problem must be possible. Hunt (1951) argued that these cases must provide a basis for an intelligent difference of opinion: "The decision-reaching process, not the decision, is the substance of the case method" (p. 183).

According to Towl (1969), cases are bounded by the requirement for a business decision. Researchers go into a company and have to discover and define an issue: they interview individuals in the firm, examine records, and may examine industry data. An issue for resolution rarely presents itself. When the issue is determined, according to Towl, the case is bounded by the data and materials needed to resolve the issue. Towl's point is an important one; that is, that cases cannot simply be reported by a survey of executives or obtained simply by interviewing them. Rather, the construction of a business case is a research task.

How Cases Are Used Pedagogically

Cases are used in a variety of ways in business schools, but mainly in two primary ways: as supplements to the course or as the mainstay of the course itself (Forrester & Oldham, 1981). The difficulty with the first approach is that "initial interest often evaporates and students come to regard case studies as a rather pointless 'gimmick'" (p. 68). Forrester and Oldham favored the second approach, which blends the cases with lectures and reading assignments.

In the literature on the business case method, there are many statements about how cases, in particular the classic cases, ought to be used in the classroom. The cases are meant to foster group discussion and analysis, and conclude with a statement for action and a prognosis for remediation, all under the nondirective guidance of the professor:

> Under the case method, the instructor functions as moderator of the case meeting. He asks such questions as he deems likely to stimulate the students' thinking and to encourage further discussion. He maintains order by recognizing the students who are to speak. And finally he decides when the point has been reached where the discussion should be concluded and summed up. (Copeland, 1958, pp. 268–269)

Cases in this field, perhaps because of their professional rather than scholarly emphasis, are rather loosely related to theory. Hunt (1951) argued that time must be allocated for the relation of the conclusions of the case class to the theory in the discipline; yet, he conceded that goals related to developing theoretical understanding are "not always reached and sometimes not even recognized" (p. 183).

Criticisms of the Case Method

The previous discussion of the business case method focused on how it has been described by the leaders in the field, primarily from Harvard Business School, but one of the major criticisms of the case method in business is that it rarely lives up to these depictions. In fact, Dooley and Skinner (1977) suggested that the use of the term *case method* in business is illusory because of the almost endless variations that can be found in business case classes. In their limited survey of business teaching, they found little of the student analysis and discussion advocated by leaders in the field: "None of the observed classes had relied primarily on student analyses and conclusions; in none had the professor played a 'non-directive' role, leaving decisions primarily to the students" (p. 281).

A study by Argyris (1980) supported the assertion that case discussions are often teacher dominated. He found that as instructors used the same case repeatedly, they hinted at the preferred solution to a problem. These findings were based on a study of case-method teachers known for their expertise with the technique.

Smith (1977) argued that despite the widespread use of the case method in business administration courses, relatively few studies have been conducted to gauge its effectiveness in reaching the objectives sought. He concluded that these studies indicate that the case method is more effective at promoting knowledge retention and application than knowledge acquisition. Further, he found several recent studies that indicated that the analysis of cases promoted problem-solving skill development. Thus, the business case method, like the case methods in law and medicine, is now coming under more careful scrutiny.

The Business Case Method and Teacher Education

The model of the case method in this field is a departure from the case methods in law and medicine in that students are expected to participate in group decision making, and the idea that there are multiple solutions is stressed. Further, there does not seem to be the pressure to cultivate a certain procedure to generate solutions, as there is in law and medicine. Students in business schools are taught to draw on eclectic sources and apply analysis and problem-solving skills to the problem at hand. Thus, in this field, the way of knowing that is being promoted appears to be much more ambiguous. Part of this ambiguity stems from the fact that the relationship of cases to theory seems to be largely a function of the discretion of the professor. If future executives are being taught to integrate their own personal knowledge and intuition with theory and research in the analysis of a business problem, then constructivist knowing may be cultivated by this method. On the other hand, if research and theory is not used to transform and enlighten the perspectives of the students, then subjective knowing might actually be promoted through this model of the case method. Further, part of the rationale for the systematic study of cases in teacher education is that the concrete detail of cases will facilitate theoretical instruction in students who are oriented toward the concrete and experiential. Here that strength of the case method is not systematically exploited.

As for the instructional goals elaborated earlier for teacher education, including the development of theoretical understanding, the fact that theoretical study is not structurally built into this case method is a major disadvantage of this model: it does not necessarily promote theoretical understanding or the disposition to bring principles to cases.

The two positive qualities of this case method versus the others discussed in this chapter are the role played by the instructor and the group nature of this method. Within the business case method, the professor is more a facilitator than a judge or examiner. Unlike the judgmental and skeptical law professor or clinical instructor, the business professor supports the group to solve business problems. This method is also less individualistic than either the legal or medical case method, since sharing and collective decision making are stressed.

In sum, although the business case method has been considered an apt precedent for teacher education, it has disadvantages, the most serious of which is the almost discretionary linkage between theory and cases.

CONCLUSION

The foremost conclusion of this chapter is that there is no such thing as "the case method." Each occupation has developed its own form of case method over time, and within that general form, variation is common. Some of this variation is attributable to the differences in the knowledge bases of the professions (see Merseth, 1991b; Shulman, 1984) and the nature of the cases in each field.

Second, in each field discussed here, cases have been used to teach practitioners to think in the specific ways that scholars believe to be productive in practice. Each case method is advanced as a means of developing a type of thinking that would prepare the practitioner to meet future problems, rather than merely covering or mastering the knowledge base. In law and medicine, this shift to an emphasis on process occurred, in part, to accommodate the growth of knowledge in these areas. It should be noted that the legal case method was criticized as a particularly slow means of covering material. Using Westbury's (1973) framework, which was described in Chapter 1, case methods generally might be characterized as high on mastery, but low on coverage.

If Nader (1978) and other critics are right about the narrowness of the thinking that is taught through the Harvard Law School's case method, then it is certainly an inappropriate model for teacher education. Given the extremely value-laden nature of their work, teachers can hardly afford to be morally aloof or insensitive to normative issues. Whereas the legal case method may serve to narrow one's vision, it would seem crucial in teacher education to find ways to use cases that would instead broaden and enrich one's view of the phenomena of practice.

Although case methods are quite different across fields, one commonality they do have is that they are a demanding form of pedagogy, for both the professor and the student. The use of case methods is difficult for the professor because engaging in Socratic discussion, or simply leading large group discussions skillfully, is difficult. Certainly, many professors would find it easier to deliver a prepared lecture. It is difficult for students because it is easier to simply take lecture notes than to engage in thoughtful discussion. Most theorists would agree, however, that discussion activities centered on important ideas are far more likely to result in meaningful learning than more passive methods.

Finally, none of the case methods surveyed in this chapter fully meets the instructional goals posited for teacher education at the conclusion of Chapter 3. Although the legal case method has the virtue of making the study of cases synonymous with the acquisition of legal theory, Socratic discussion is unlikely to promote the epistemological growth of women. Case methods in both medicine and law promote separate procedural knowing, which, it has been argued, does not lend itself to the field of teaching. Finally, the business case method has the advantage of embracing a nonjudgmental, facilitative role for the professor, but the looseness between theory and case analysis makes this an unlikely candidate as a model for teacher education, where the development of theoretical understanding is key. In the next chapter, a case method for teacher education will be proposed that will meet the instructional goals of promoting theoretical understanding, developing the intellectual growth of women, and strengthening the disposition to bring principles to cases.

5

The Case Method in
Teacher Education

Let the main objective of this, our didactic, be as follows: To
seek and find a method of instruction, by which teachers may
teach less, but learners may learn more.
— *The Great Didactic of Comenius*,
as cited in Cockerill, 1948, p. 128

One of the integral aspects of the reform of legal and medical education was the ushering in of a new kind of pedagogy. In each of
these fields and later in business, academic leaders argued that
students must study firsthand the concrete phenomena of practice. Further, they argued that this experience must be active
rather than passive, and scientific rather than empirical. The "scientific" case method was soon adapted to other fields as well, such
as social work and nursing. Because these occupations, like teaching, have historically been women's professions, teacher educators
may find their case methods more illuminating than the case
methods in traditionally masculine fields. Towle's (1954) remarkable volume describing the social-work education program at the
University of Chicago supports this idea.

In that work, Towle (1954) described the careful use and se-
quencing of cases to meet the affective and cognitive goals of the
program. The affective objectives included the "development of
appropriate feelings and attitudes" (p. 234). That this program included such instructional goals is itself a departure from traditional programs in the fields of law, medicine, and business that
typically train practitioners not to let their feelings get in the way
of their practice.

Towle (1954) explained that the study of cases was carefully
arranged to induce increasingly complex intellectual and emo-

tional responses from the social work student, including the capacity to empathize with the client:

> One begins where the learner is. One does not make an unrealistic intellectual and emotional demand. The student is undertaking to help people. A first essential is to understand the person needing help, to understand at least something of the meaning of his problem to him and the meaning of this experience of having to ask for and take help. This demands some feeling with the person. It implies putting one's self into his shoes and viewing his situation as far as possible through his eyes, while retaining one's own vision (p. 290).

The language Towle used here strikingly echoes Belenky et al.'s (1986) description of connected procedural knowing. The case sequence in this program began with cases in which the clients were "least strange" (p. 290) and with whom the students could most readily identify. The program progressed to cases in which the clients were not primarily the victims of circumstance, but were more exceptional. Towle wrote that the purpose of this arrangement was to produce in the student in the early stage of the program an ability to identify with the client without ambivalence, to develop in the student a feeling that "there but for the grace of God go I" (p. 290). Thus, based on Towle's description, the cultivation of a form of connected knowing was an explicit goal of this program. Perhaps Towle's work, as well as the contributions of other educators who use cases in programs that historically have served women, can be more helpful models for teacher education than the predominantly masculine fields reviewed in the previous chapter.

In Chapters 1–4 of this work, I argued that a case-based pedagogy holds promise for teacher education. The task of this chapter is to present an outline of a case method for teacher education, and it begins with an effort to place this work in the context of other works on case methods in teacher education. The remainder of the chapter is devoted to explicating a proposal for a case method that I call "case construction." It includes a discussion of some premises of the method and a presentation of the method itself, suggesting some qualities successful cases are likely to possess and describing anticipated outcomes. Finally, some challenges facing teacher educators interested in teaching with cases are explored.

HISTORICAL ATTEMPTS TO USE THE CASE METHOD

D. Henryetta Sperle's (1933) account of the teacher education program at New Jersey State Teachers College at Montclair describes perhaps the only use of cases for the preparation of teachers at the program level. Her work explicated the program at Montclair during the period 1925–1932. According to Sperle (1933), Montclair's student teachers were asked to collect and record their problems in the classroom on index cards or other types of forms. Typically, the data to be reported included a brief statement of the problem; a fuller, more detailed description of the difficulty; attempted solutions; and finally, the solution reached or progress achieved.

Sperle reported that the collection of the case problems served two major purposes. First, it was believed to be helpful to students who were experiencing difficulties in their practice teaching.

> When the students returned for campus conferences opportunities were provided for those who had common problems (1) to meet together with one or more staff members who could best assist in thinking through the difficulty, or (2) to observe and discuss a demonstration lesson which had been arranged to help clarify a fundamental principle or a technique. (p. 26)

Apart from helping candidates with their classroom problems, the second purpose of collecting case problems was to gather material for use in professional education courses. That is, the case records provided incidents for discussion in methods courses and foundations courses. The case cards were collected and classified in the central office so that they could be used at a future time.

To the extent that the collected problems and solutions served as precedents, this form of the case method shared some characteristics of the legal case method. Solutions that appeared to work well in the past could provide guidance for solving current problems with similar characteristics. On the other hand, when the collected problems were used as a basis of discussion in class, the use of the case records appears to have resembled something closer to the business case method—they were the basis of shared decision making and discussion.

It is interesting to note that the way of knowing embraced

through this form of the case method is separate procedural knowing, as students had to record the data pertaining to the case and the attempted solutions. This case method contrasts sharply with the one advanced by Towle (1954) that was described at the beginning of this chapter. As noted there, one of the explicit aims of the social work education program she described was the cultivation of proper emotional responses. Sperle's (1933) account does not include any affective goals for the case method developed at Montclair.

Questionnaires filled out by both teacher candidates and faculty members at Montclair in 1932 revealed that the case method was highly valued by both groups. The candidates reported that it helped them to define and solve classroom problems, and the faculty believed that the case technique was useful in practica and in keeping the teacher education faculty close to the real world of the public schools, among other benefits (Sperle, 1933). Pennoyer (1928) offers an account of this program from a student's perspective.

Although Sperle's work is informative, it leaves unanswered broader questions about the efficacy of this form of the case method. Were teachers who were educated at Montclair better or different in some way than teachers educated elsewhere? Also, there is apparently no record of what happened to the program.

There is little evidence that a case method has been institutionalized at sites other than the New Jersey State Teacher's College at Montclair; however, it is clear that the idea of using cases in teacher education programs and for teacher supervision has been of interest to a number of teacher educators over the last 75 years. The faculty of the Harvard Graduate School of Education considered—and rejected—the implementation of a case-based pedagogy there in the 1920s. The case method was apparently viewed as inappropriate for the field of teaching. In addition, the faculty had difficulty reaching a consensus on the goals of the school's programs and thus what purpose cases could fulfill (Merseth, 1991b). The publication of case collections—texts consisting entirely of cases—have appeared throughout this century. See, for example, Anderson, Barr, and Bush (1925), Brackenbury (1959), Greenwood, Good, and Siegel (1971), Ladd and Sayres (1962), Perry and Perry (1969), and Waples (1927).

RECENT SCHOLARSHIP ON CASE METHODS

Recent scholarship on case methods in teacher education reflects the fact that teacher educators have made little progress in
reaching a consensus regarding their goals and purposes since the
faculty at the Harvard Graduate School of Education first dismissed the idea of a case-based pedagogy. The proposals for case
use are varied and reflect the wide range of conceptual orientations found among teacher education programs (see A. McAninch,
1991; Merseth, 1991b; Sykes & Bird, 1992). As Merseth (1991b)
correctly pointed out, a "program's conceptual orientation should
influence their choice of cases" (p. 246). On the other hand, her
assertion that "such diversity can be healthy" (p. 246) if the orientation of the program is clear and matched with their use of the
case method disregards criteria other than clarity and consistency
in the justification of teacher education practices.

One way of thinking about proposals for the case method is to
ask which "way of knowing" they advance (A. McAninch, 1991). For
example, the casebook by Kowalski, Weaver, and Henson (1990)
embraces a received knowing perspective in which the teacher is
viewed as someone who solves narrow technical problems using
knowledge received by others. Greenwood and Parkay (1989) develop cases as a vehicle for cultivating a type of separate procedural knowing—one in which a solution to a teaching problem is
the result of a six-step process that explicitly links theory to case
analysis. Other proposals for using cases advance the idea that the
most important knowledge for teaching is developed or resides in
the practice setting. These proposals, which give emphasis to the
importance of firsthand experience, craft, and the particularism
of teaching, support subjective knowing to various degrees (Carter,
1988, 1990; Merseth, 1991a; Shulman, Colbert, Kemper, & Dmytriw, 1990).

In turning to recent scholarship on case methods that can
contribute to constructed knowing, the work of L. Shulman (1986,
1992) is very helpful. Shulman has emphasized the idea of using
cases to teach theory—of having a case literature that is "profoundly theoretical." Shulman's repudiation of a craft basis for
teaching echoes Dewey's rejection of practices that have only an
empirical sanction. Shulman, like Dewey (1904), views the development of judgment and theoretical knowledge as key to the pro-
fessionalization of teaching. In fact, Shulman's insistence on a case
method that is profoundly theoretical and that gives candidates

practice in bringing principles to instances echoes Dewey's plea that teachers learn to observe "theoretically." His conceptualization of a case method for teacher education (1986), however, presupposes both theoretical knowledge and development beyond the clinical and subjectivist orientations described in Chapters 1 and 2. The case method that I advance below, which I call the "case construction" method, can prepare students to engage in the kind of thinking that L. Shulman sees as fundamental in teaching.

Both Dewey (1904) and L. Shulman (1986) argue that the teacher's capacity to observe the particular through a theoretical perspective—and the capacity to use those principles in an intelligent manner—is key to professional practice. Shulman's emphasis on bringing principles to cases and developing the capacity to arbitrate between principles reflects the influence of Joseph Schwab, with whom Shulman studied at the University of Chicago. Schwab's thinking, in turn, was heavily influenced by his colleague, John Dewey (Westbury & Wilkof, 1978). It is not surprising then, that the proposal described below, which is conceived of as a steppingstone to the intellectual habits Dewey (1904) believed teachers should possess, relies heavily on the work of Schwab and L. Shulman. In the following section, the premises underlying the "case construction" method are explicated.

PREMISES OF THE CASE CONSTRUCTION METHOD

This section has two goals: to outline some of the assumptions or premises upon which my proposal for a case method rests and to explain how the study of cases may facilitate the attainment of the aims posited for this methodology that were advanced in Chapter 4.

Theories as Lenses

Theory enters practice indirectly through the judgment of the teacher. In other words, theories are lenses the teacher can use to observe concrete phenomena (Schwab, 1978b), or, as Shulman (1986) put it, theories are conceptual apparatuses that are imposed on an incident. Rarely are teacher candidates given the opportunity to look through theoretical perspectives at a focal point. As a consequence, theories tend to remain abstract and ultimately fail to broaden or enlighten the judgment of teachers (Tom, 1984).

Theories, as lenses through which to interpret the phenomena of practice, can be powerful instruments for the teacher. In fact, Dewey (1929a) once wrote that "theory is in the end . . . the most practical of all things" (p. 17). Theories provide an economy to observation and often provide terms and concepts that can be put into use (Schwab, 1978a). Theory can be defined as "an abstract body of concepts that serves as a basis for practice" (Shermis, 1967, p. 22). Theory may explain or describe educational phenomena, provide a hypothesis for redressing a situation, or help provide insight into the moral or ethical issues involved in a particular circumstance. Shermis also suggested that theory may provide assistance in evaluating an educational outcome or assessing results.

Theoretical understanding allows individuals to go beyond the trial and error of empirical thinking. Even good theories, however, suffer from at least two weaknesses: their subject matter is necessarily limited and the view they afford of any single event is truncated (Schwab, 1978a). Schwab noted that sociological theory concerns one subject matter, whereas psychological theory stakes claim to another. Each claims its own turf for study, demarcating the boundaries of the discipline. Further, as Schwab stated, within each discipline competing theories offer only a partial view of any phenomenon, drawing attention to some elements and overlooking others:

> Partiality of view is exemplified by the Freudian treatment of personality after the analogue of a developing, differentiating organism (a treatment which makes it extremely difficult to deal directly with problems of interpersonal relations). It is equally visible in interpersonal theories which make it difficult to deal with autogenous behaviors and feelings. (p. 296)

Schwab made the point that although theories as lenses sharpen our view of certain features of an incident, they necessarily turn our attention away from others: "We not only seek what it tells us to seek, we do not seek and only rarely note what it does *not* instruct us to search out" (1978b, p. 333). The idea advanced in Chapter 3 regarding "convenient defect of vision" (Miller, 1977) is relevant here. Some individuals may intentionally adopt an ideological perspective that affords a truncated view in order to protect their own interests. Each lens can afford only a partial view, be it insightful and powerful or cloudy. Regardless of how perceptive a certain theory may be, the exclusive reliance on it results in an attenuated view.

The problem then, for teacher educators, as Dewey (1904), Schwab (1978b), and Shulman (1986) noted, is how to help candidates achieve facility with a range of theories and use them intelligently in a given concrete instance. Because educational problems are multidisciplinary, teacher candidates need knowledge not only of competing theories within a single discipline, but of rival theories across disciplines. Although Shulman is interested in using a case method to develop strategic knowledge—that is, the ability to arbitrate between competing theories—my initial aim is to use cases to build the capacity to look through various lenses at a focal point.

Cases as Theoretical Constructions

Shulman's (1986) discussion of the components of the knowledge base of teaching provides one of the most helpful conceptualizations of what constitutes a case and case knowledge. Case knowledge, according to Shulman, is "knowledge of specific, well-documented, and richly described events" (p. 11). A necessary condition for possessing this form of knowledge, he wrote, is theoretical knowledge:

> A case, properly understood, is not simply the report of an event or incident. To call something a case is to make a theoretical claim—to argue that it is a "case of something," or to argue that it is an instance of a larger class. (p. 11)

Thus, case knowledge and theoretical knowledge are intricately linked. For example, the effort to discover what illness a patient "is a case of" is a diagnostic task that requires theoretical knowledge. For this reason, the translation of a problem or an event into a case is a theoretical task. Shulman pointed out that the interpretation of events without theoretical knowledge is "mere anecdote, a parable without a moral" (p. 12). Of course, the reverse relationship is also true: the possession of theoretical knowledge depends on the knowledge of instances that are subsumed by those abstract categories or conceptual frameworks.

Shulman adds that while cases may be reports of events, they are "cases" because they represent theoretical knowledge:

What a given occasion is "a case of" is not immediately apparent
from the account itself. Generalizability does not inhere in the
case, but in the conceptual apparatus of the explicator. An event
can be described; a case must be explicated, interpreted, argued, dissected, and reassembled. . . . Hence, there is no real
case knowledge without theoretical understanding. (p. 12)

Thus, cases are phenomena of practice or events that are theoretically interpreted. They are "documented (or portrayed) occasions
or sets of occasions with their boundaries marked off, their borders drawn" (p. 12). The boundaries of a case and the data included in a case are shaped by the theoretical apparatus through
which the event is interpreted. Because cases are events that have
been theoretically constructed, I will use the term *case* to refer to
the product of a theoretical inquiry, much as a legal case is the
product of a legal proceeding. The term *narrative* will be used to
refer to a description of an incident or event that can be formu-
lated into a case through theoretical interpretation and inquiry,
although it is important to point out that stories or descriptions
of events comprise only a subset of the items in experience that
could potentially become cases.

Cases for Developing Theoretical Understanding

One of the contributions a case method can make to teacher
education is related to teaching theory to subjective and received
knowers. Leaving the developmental aspect aside for the moment,
case analysis can be a valuable means of teaching theory for the
following reasons.

One of the deficiencies of the traditional way in which theory
has been taught in teacher education programs is that it is often
divorced from practice settings and concrete instances (Tom,
1984). The teacher candidate may master theory in the abstract,
but gain no facility or disposition to observe instances in a theoretical way. It is legitimate to wonder how deeply a student knows a
given doctrine without the capacity to bring it to bear on a concrete instance. Studying cases can provide opportunities for this
linkage—for not only mastering the lens, but practicing looking
through it to some field. Because theoretical understanding hinges
on the knowledge of cases that are members of that theoretical class, the study of cases is a means of building theoretical
knowledge.

Case analysis can also help obviate two common reactions to

typical survey courses in which a group of theories related to a particular phenomenon is presented serially (Schwab, 1978b). Schwab lamented that these courses are typically met by two types of reactions from students. On the one hand, some students are anxious to determine which theory is "right":

> The whole burden of their education . . . has been a collection of unique solutions to sharply separated problems and of single bodies of "fact" about each of many isolated subject matters. With such a background, students are quite unprepared to recognize the character of theoretic pluralism, much less cope with it. (pp. 334–335)

In short, when students' school experience has been dominated by convergent problems, it is hardly surprising that at the college level the habit of looking for the right answer is deeply ingrained. As discussed in Chapter 2, a plea for "the answer" is symptomatic of received knowers who cannot tolerate the ambiguity of such an array of constructions, each forwarded by an expert. For students who believe there is a single answer, Schwab contended, such surveys "are neither understood nor believed" (p. 335).

A second reaction to survey courses, Schwab argued, is that each theory is taken to be as valid as the other:

> Each member of a conspectus has evidence and argument to support it. Each is espoused by one substantial voice of authority. Each, therefore, must be, in some sense, right. Each, then, deserves respect and mastery (1978b, p. 335).

Schwab suggested that students who react in this way leave a survey course believing that whichever theory they pick out of the conspectus will be as valid as another: it is simply a matter of personal preference. This reaction is reminiscent of subjective knowing, in which learners are unable to apply rational procedures for weighing truth claims and rely instead on personal experience and instinct. Further, we might well imagine some students adding, "They have their theories, I have mine," discounting the survey all together. In other words, whereas Schwab argued that some students react to a conspectus with the "all theories are equally valid" point of view and in the end, pick one theory out of the survey, it is alternatively plausible for students to reject all the theories in the conspectus in favor of a theory derived from firsthand experience.

Certainly, as Schwab maintained, these outcomes are undesirable: the power of theories as instrumentalities, as ways of perceiving that are necessarily partial and incomplete, is lost on both groups. How may a case method alter the situation? Schwab (1978b) suggested that case analysis may provide a means of demonstrating that theories are not matters of right or wrong, but that each theory brings something to its concrete subject matter. In other words, the presentation of cases would be a "means by which students can discover the various powers of perception which a variety of theories can confer" (p. 336). For example, if students read a particular narrative and come to understand that Thomas Jefferson's theory of education highlights certain concepts, such as the "natural distribution of talent and virtue," whereas Dewey's theory of democratic education gives emphasis to others, the tendency to feel the need to choose one theory may well be undercut.

Finally, there is one last reason why a case method can be a useful tool for teaching theory in teacher education. Highly detailed narratives may address the subjective, clinical consciousness of many teacher candidates where abstract propositional prose alone does not. Although the qualities of narratives that are most potentially fruitful for the purposes forwarded here are described below, it is important to point out that well-written descriptions of real, concrete situations and contexts may reach teacher candidates who are overwhelmingly oriented toward the practice setting and toward the experiential. Whereas these students may be highly resistant to abstract theorizing and experts, the study of concrete instances may be a means of making theoretical studies palatable to this group.

A case method can be useful in teaching theory, then, because it can pull the abstract down to the level of practice; it can provide, in Schwab's (1978b) terms, an apparatus by which teacher candidates can examine the relative contributions of an array of theories to the understanding of a particular situation; and finally, cases may address the experiential and practical orientation of teacher candidates to a greater extent than abstract textbook prose. In the next sections, the contribution that case analysis can make to teachers' epistemological development will be examined.

Cases as a Tool for Epistemological Development

A case method can also be an important methodology for promoting development because it can encourage students to engage in procedural knowing. Previously, I cited Belenky et al.'s (1986) story of the art history student's analysis of paintings as an example of an experience that prompts students to engage in procedural thinking. In fact, the analysis of paintings according to various criteria is a form of the case method. This pedagogy encourages students to focus on the qualities of the object, rather than on their intuitive, wholistic, or emotional reaction to it. It cultivates separate procedural knowing by placing distance between the object and the self.

In much the same way, case analysis in teacher education can provide a challenge to a subjective knower's perspective. But instead of encouraging separate procedural knowing, as the art history professor had done, the case construction method seeks connected procedural knowing. By insisting that teacher candidates expand their own personal reaction to a narrative, at least temporarily, and look at it through Skinner's eyes, or from Piaget's point of view, the subjective outlook is broadened. Connected procedural knowing as a perspective, it may also be recalled, has the pedagogical advantage of exploiting the subjective belief that everyone is entitled to their own view (Belenky et al., 1986). A case method that cultivates connected knowing has a distinct upper hand in classrooms where a large number of students may be subjective knowers at the outset. Finally, connected procedural knowing is emphasized for one additional reason. Whereas evidence suggests that women are socialized to be connected, men are socialized to be the opposite: autonomous and independent. Since teaching, like social work, is a practice in which empathy and connection with students are fundamental, men may generally need practice in developing those affective skills. Thus, the case construction method, through the introduction of theories as points of view that are to be understood and temporarily believed rather than doubted, is aimed at encouraging the connected procedural knowing perspective.

In Chapter 2, I noted that the vast majority of teacher candidates are likely to be subjective knowers, whereas many others are likely to be received knowers. These latter individuals have not yet developed an inner voice, a sense of self that enables them to listen to or assert their own ideas. Received knowing shares with procedural knowing a putting aside of the inner self in favor of other ways of knowing. Thus, received knowers may be capable of developing toward the position of procedural knowing, which essentially involves receiving knowledge from a procedure rather than from an authority figure. For this reason, case analysis may have developmental benefits for these students as well. Having described why the study of cases may be useful for teaching theory and for spurring epistemological development, the discussion will turn to a specific procedure for the use of cases.

PRESENTATION OF THE CASE CONSTRUCTION METHOD

This proposal for use of the case construction method has three aims:

1. To develop theoretical understanding—that is, to help teacher candidates look through the lenses of different doctrines
2. To help candidates move toward an epistemological orientation that integrates the personal and the scientific—that is, toward the perspective described by Dewey (1904) and Belenky et al. (1986), which the latter calls "constructed knowing"
3. To strengthen the disposition to bring principles to the concrete phenomena of practice

In developing this proposal, I borrowed heavily from Schwab's "polyfocal conspectus" (1978b), a methodology he devised for "imparting to students a measure of inclination toward and competence for examining educational situations and problems in more than one set of terms" (p. 356). The additional emphasis of the case construction methodology is the cultivation of connected procedural knowing in order to promote epistemological development.

The Procedure

The method would begin as Schwab described the first phase of polyfocal conspectus. Students would begin by studying a particular doctrine that is a member of a group of competing theories. For example, a philosophy of education course could be designed around theories of the nature of the learner (see Bruner, 1985), perhaps starting with Locke and the tabula rasa doctrine. Other surveys might form around the problem of values education, ranging from character education approaches to Gilligan (1982), Kohlberg (1981), Kozol (1990), Noddings (1984), and Raths,

Harmin, and Simon (1978) (see Chapter 6). In a course on curriculum, surveys of theories could form around each of the four teaching tasks described by Westbury (1973) and discussed in Chapter 1. For example, theories of classroom management ranging from Skinnerian approaches to less authoritarian doctrines could be included. Because there are competing theories in every area of educational studies, the development of surveys need not be limited to one or two courses in a teacher education program.

Connected procedural knowing hinges on a process of empathy—of learning not only how to look through a new lens, but also how that lens developed (Belenky et al., 1986)—it is therefore important that each theory be presented with information about its source. The inclusion of this information addresses students who are subjectively oriented because it ties the source of ideas to broader cultural experience and even the personal experience of the theorist.

Depending on the students, either primary or secondary sources could be relied on as source material. To make this phase of case construction an active learning experience for students, didactic methods should be used sparingly. Other methods, such as small group work, discussion, concept mapping, and independent library research could be utilized during this segment. Ideally, the teacher would primarily play the role of facilitator, rather than source of knowledge.

After the entire class attains a basic understanding of the general concepts and ideas of a theoretical perspective, attention would be turned to a narrative. Following Shulman (1986), a description of an event is not a case until a conceptual apparatus has been imposed on it. Thus, the construction of a case from a description of a particular instance is the next part of the procedure.

At the outset, it is important to point out that starting with a doctrine and then turning to a problem of practice is diametrically opposed to most other case method proposals in teacher education. Others argue that the case generates interest and sets the problem: if developing problem-solving skill is an aim of the method, then it makes very good sense to present students with the kinds of problems they are likely to face and to give them practice in solving them. This proposal for case method starts with theory because one of its aims is to develop theoretical understanding, not problem-solving skill. The idea here, as in Schwab (1978b), is to have students get a clear *partial* view of the narrative, not to have them get a holistic, undisciplined view and then try to fracture that whole picture with a theoretical point of view. For this reason, the doctrine should be presented first, and then a narrative should be presented.

Following Schwab (1978b), the discussion would focus on picking out those features of the narrative that make it a case of a particular theory and ignoring those that do not, or in Schwab's terms, "transforming the doctrine into a view" (p. 356). In other words, by looking through the lens of the theory, that is, taking on a particular theoretical perspective, students are engaged in constructing a case from the narrative through the process of connected knowing.

If the theories under study, for example, were those included in Bruner's survey of theories of the learner, the discussion leader may start out by asking what might Locke see in this case, what would he attend to, what would he think was important? How would he view this teacher's activity or explain this child's behavior? The aim of this discussion is not to criticize Locke's theory or to explain what one thinks of Locke's theory from a personal point of view, but to assume that he is credible and to gain as full a Lockean understanding of the narrative as possible.

Again following Schwab (1978b), the question might also be asked, are certain aspects of Locke's theory not addressed by the narrative? That is, what additional information not included in the narrative might be collected in order to gain an even deeper Lockean view of this instance? In this way, the narrative is transformed into a case of Locke's doctrine through its theoretical interpretation according to this perspective. It should be emphasized that some theories may illuminate certain events with great power and insight—and even provide guidance about a course of action that might be attempted to redress a problem. Other theories applied to the same situation may afford less understanding and less help. Thus, the case construction process is experimental in nature, encouraging teachers to try one theoretical perspective and then another.

The next unit would proceed in the same way, with students studying a competing theory to the one first presented, perhaps Dewey's view of the learner. After the theory and its background have been studied through a variety of methods, the same narrative would be reinterpreted. This time, the object would be to construct a case of Dewey's doctrine from the narrative, using ideas central to his view of the learner as an active participant in his or her own learning.

This process would be repeated—imposing theories on the narrative in order to construct cases—as many times as there are theories to be presented in the unit. The last exercise of the survey, after students have had practice at viewing the narrative through these theoretical perspectives, would be to compare and contrast the cases that were constructed through this process. The class can then weigh the strengths and weaknesses of the theoretical perspectives. The discussion should include not only what the theoretical perspectives say about the case, but what the case says about the theories. If a theoretical perspective seems inadequate in some way, then the students can consider what that means for the theory. It may also be useful at the conclusion of the unit to introduce a different narrative, one that may lead to different conclusions than the first one to underscore the idea that some theoretical perspectives may be helpful in certain circumstances and not in others.

The Narratives

In the professions of medicine and law, cases are marked off from one another and are generated in practice. In the field of business, the boundaries of a case are drawn by the nature of a problem discovered in the field. If, as Shulman (1986) wrote, "cases are documented (or portrayed) occasions or sets of occasions with their boundaries marked off, their borders drawn" (p. 12), it is unclear in the field of education what will serve as such occasions. For example, is the unit of analysis the student? The classroom? An individual teacher? Some educational problems address whole communities or even the entire country.

As noted above, any and all concrete phenomena of practice are potentially cases—not just narratives. Grade books, a test, a student teacher evaluation, school district financial data, all of these artifacts are potentially cases. Yet, for the pedagogical purposes advanced here, a narrative is more likely to address the concrete and experiential orientation of the subjective knower. Ultimately, it is important to help teacher candidates find as much meaning in good data as in good narratives, but that requires development beyond subjective knowing. For this reason, this discussion will center on narratives.

In keeping with the conception of teacher education embraced in Chapter 3, it is important that the narratives facilitate the study of profound ideas in education, rather than simply address narrow technical concerns. In other words, although a narrative about a teacher candidate searching for a teaching position could be treated theoretically as an occasion to study theories of school norms and culture (Kowalski, Weaver, & Henson, 1989), there are probably other occasions that could provide a more provocative study of these theories. For example, a teacher candidate who recently graduated from Knox College in Galesburg, Illinois, completed her student teaching in an inner city Chicago high school in which gang activity seemed to dominate student life. In her narrative, entitled "No Colors," she described in great detail how the norms embraced by the staff in this school prevented an acknowledgment of the violent reality of their students' lives. This narrative begs theoretical explanation: What would explain these circumstances? How are these norms maintained? What are the consequences for the students? What are the consequences of these norms for novice teachers? Thus, good occasions for the purpose of promoting theoretical understanding will present profound issues in education that readily transcend technical concerns. They may describe teachers, students, classroom contexts, and curricula, giving more emphasis to teachers and students in a certain instance, perhaps emphasizing curricula in another.

In addition, there is a consensus among scholars of the case method that narratives that describe real events are better than those that are fictional. For example, Leftwich (1981) pointed out that students generally respond with more interest to cases that describe "real world" events. There are several ways to bolster the genuineness of cases. One way is to include realia related to the event in the narrative. These might include newspaper clippings, letters, and school documents and records, generated by the event. For example, Ladd and Sayres (1962) in a case about the suspension of a teacher, included correspondence between the parties in the narrative. These documents added a sense of reality and drama to the case.

Another feature good narratives should have is that they ought to be as experiential as possible: they ought to be vivid and compelling. This quality is intended to bolster interest in case construction, but also to address the subjective knowers' orientation toward the experiential. Some narratives do not invite the reader to become involved in the events. For example, Brackenbury's casebook (1959) contains brief descriptions of classroom problems that are relatively devoid of detail or context, followed by accounts of how teachers of various educational philosophies might attack the problem. He concludes with fictional interviews with each teacher. Although the problems Brackenbury sketched are no doubt encountered by millions of teachers everyday in the public schools, the rather shallow descriptions of the problems, plus the fictional accounts, are enough to diminish any sense of identification with the teacher or his or her situation. The cases in this text remain a secondhand experience.

Next, narratives should be sufficiently broad and complex that real effort must be exerted to impose the theory on them. In other words, the narrative collection ought not to consist of a Dewey case, in which experience and the project method are underscored, and a Skinner case, in which responses and behaviors are highlighted. Writing cases in this way would be solving the problem for the students. Instead, narratives ought to be so broad that any one of them could be fruitfully used as a focus point for a wide array of educational theories. The narratives, if they are going to be used as a focal point for a succession of competing theoretical views—not just of one discipline, but of various areas—must be rich enough to accommodate multiple theories of different subject matters.

Finally, narratives should convey a sense of closure. Because the object of this case method is not to teach problem solving or decision making, the narrative should not be open-ended, but convey a sense of closure.

Expected Outcomes

The expected outcomes of the case construction method are threefold. First, it is anticipated that teacher candidates would develop a solid grasp of the theories covered in the course through the construction of cases. The theoretical understanding developed through this method, it is expected, would be deeper than that which originally results from survey courses taught without narratives. It provides an opportunity for students to develop knowledge of cases that exemplify the theories under study.

The case construction method also develops the disposition to view concrete instances through the lenses of different theories, that is, to develop a tendency to observe in a principled way, as Dewey advocated in his 1904 essay. The ability to do so is necessary if one is to develop the kind of judgment Shulman (1986) called "strategic wisdom."

Third, this method, because it is procedural and focuses attention away from the self to an object, may help subjective and received knowers to develop toward the position of procedural knowledge. During the analysis of a particular instance, the focus is on the concrete situation through a lens, the point of view of someone else. This process prompts students to try this new way of looking. Perhaps if students are given many such opportunities, they may find their epistemological orientation unsatisfying and move to a new orientation toward knowing. This development is important because Belenky et al. (1986) found that constructivist knowers, those who integrated their subjective perspective with rational thought, were often procedural knowers before adopting the constructivist position. This constructivist orientation coincides with the perspective Dewey (1904) advocated for teachers; thus, to the extent that Dewey's conception is embraced, the development of procedural knowing is of utmost importance.

DISADVANTAGES OF CASE METHODS

The last consideration of this chapter is of the potential disadvantages of using this or other case methods. One of its liabilities, as with all case methods, is that it is a relatively slow means of covering material. If there is pressure to include in the syllabus five areas of study, each with several competing theories, this method probably will not allow completion of all of the material. From the point of view of Westbury's model, described in Chapter 1, case methods tend to sacrifice some coverage of subject matter for the sake of mastery.

Further, there is some question as to whether a single professor can "go it alone" with any case method: "If it is squeezed into the programme of study once a term, for instance, students . . . may come to treat case study rather like a separate subject or course, and as either entertainment or distraction" (Leftwich, 1981, p. 52). Leftwich argued that to be successful, there must be some commitment to the case method at the departmental level. In fact, the case construction method described above is intended to be the first in a series of experiences with cases. Certainly, if case construction constitutes 3 hours of instruction out of the 120 hours required for graduation, the aims of the method probably will not be realized. Still, if one professor attempts the method and it proves enormously successful, there is a chance that others will try it as well. The anticipated outcomes of case use seem well worth the sacrifice in coverage and the effort to organize programs or sequences centered on case methods.

Further, Shulman (1992) raises another interesting issue associated with case method teaching. One of the disadvantages he cites is that the lessons students draw from reading cases may be overgeneralized. A moral drawn from a parable may become in the student mind a fixed rule. For example, in one of the narratives in Chapter 6, a principal lies to a group of students. If teacher candidates learn from this case that one should never lie to students, then that would be an overgeneralization and would not prepare them well to think through situations when lying to students may be morally justified. The very danger of overgeneralizations is found in the same quality that makes cases useful as a form of knowledge: they are vivid and memorable. More research on this issue would be extremely valuable.

Finally, case methods are generally considered to be a difficult teaching strategy. Like other discussion methods, it requires a great amount of skill on the part of the instructor because it can't be planned out in advance. If students respond with analyses that are unanticipated, it requires thinking on the spot. Worse yet, if students are altogether unresponsive, no preplanned lecture can be relied upon. As with all student-centered instruction, case methods are dependent in large part on the students and their willingness to be prepared and participate in discussion. Of course, if a certain class seems resistant to this method, consideration of alternatives is necessary.

CONCLUSION

Proposals for the use of cases range from developing a literature that may help stabilize teacher education programs to developing strategic knowledge. The case construction methodology forwarded here, which is drawn from Schwab's concept of polyfocal conspectus, involves the use of cases to provide a focal point for theoretical perspectives. As theories are serially imposed on concrete, vivid instances, those narratives are transformed through analysis and interpretation into cases.

The aims of this procedure are theoretical understanding; the development of the skills and dispositions to look through the lenses of various theories to an instance, that is, to construct a case; and finally, the development of connected procedural knowing, which is the epistemological orientation desirable in teaching.

The disadvantages associated with this method are overshadowed by the possible benefits it may afford. In the next chapter, examples of narratives and conspectuses will be offered, along with analyses that illustrate the case construction method.

6
The Uses of Narratives and Theoretical Perspectives

In this final chapter, three examples of case materials are provided. A complete case construction would include a *narrative,* at least one *theoretical perspective,* and the *theoretical interpretation* of the narrative. All three of the narratives are followed by suggested references for theoretical perspectives; in addition, a theoretical interpretation of the first narrative is included as an example of the type of analysis advocated in Chapter 5.

In the opening section of this chapter, the discussion focuses on the selection and organization of case materials. In the remainder of the chapter, the case construction materials are presented. According to the methodology advanced in Chapter 5, teacher educators would present the first theoretical perspective, and then alternate between the narrative and the remaining lenses. For the sake of organizational clarity, I have not followed that pattern in this chapter. This chapter presents potential case materials for the case construction process, not an account of how the methodology actually would proceed. Teachers educators can read the narratives and survey the theoretical perspectives to gain an idea of the kinds of materials that could be used. The narratives and theoretical perspectives herein are meant to suggest and illustrate, but do not begin to exhaust the possibilities of the case construction process.

The first narrative, "Theory and Practice in Education," concerns the perspectives of teachers and a university professor toward theory. "Teaching Democracy" is a lengthier and more detailed account. It may be used to consider theoretical issues pertaining to evaluation, curriculum theory, ethics in school administration, and the teacher's role in a democracy, among others. Finally, the third narrative, "No Conscience," describes issues related to the moral education of an alienated student.

DEVELOPMENT OF THE NARRATIVES

The form and content of the narratives in this chapter were selected and developed with the three aims of the case construction method in mind. Therefore, the first question in developing these materials was, "What theoretical understandings do I want to teach?" In courses that I have taught at Knox College and elsewhere, a multidisciplinary, liberal, and critical approach to the study of education has been a cornerstone of the teacher education programs (see, for example, Beyer, 1991). Thus, the narratives were designed to be a focal point for an array of theoretical perspectives in various disciplines—especially sociology, philosophy, psychology, and the history of education.

One of the issues related to narrative development is whether or not they should present problems, as the business case method does. In her thoughtful dissertation, Boyd (1985) described how she developed cases. She wrote that the issues she selected had to "be problems of a certain nature: non-routine and complex problems" (p. 48). She suggested that problems in this Deweyan sense promote reflection—they challenge habit and routine. One of the difficulties with saying that the narratives should pose problems or challenge beliefs is that what is perceived as a problem is dependent on the prior knowledge and value commitments one brings to a case, as well as one's way of knowing. This is a key point of Chapter 3. In that chapter, for example, the unfulfilled aspirations of the junior high school students that Grant and Sleeter (1986) met in their research were generally not a problem for the teachers and administrators who worked in the school— with a few exceptions. However, the idea that the school did not serve the interests of these minority students well was problematic for Grant and Sleeter.

For the purposes of this work, it is not necessary that the narratives explicitly pose a conflict or problem: what should be problematic is the theoretical interpretation of each narrative. Thus, the tension involves, in Shulman's terms (1986), determining what a given narrative "is a case of" (p. 12) and the explication and interpretation of a narrative in light of theoretical perspectives. It is this process that yields case knowledge and the disposition to bring principles to cases and to reflect on their power to illuminate educational phenomena.

SELECTION OF THE THEORETICAL PERSPECTIVES

The references to theoretical work that follow the narratives were chosen as examples because they forward important intellectual ideas that are worth teaching. Many competing theories addressing a wide array of subject matter would be suitable for this process.

It is important to point out that in surveying the research on the case method in teacher education, it appears as if far more attention is currently focused on the development of cases than on the theoretical perspectives or understandings they represent. I have argued elsewhere that the identification of theories to teach and cases to accompany them must go hand in hand (McAninch, 1991). Case methods in other fields, I believe, flourished in part because important theoretical lessons could be taught through the method.

I have arranged the references to theoretical perspectives following each case in an order that ranges roughly, in my view, from those that are most likely to be familiar or compatible to the ideology students are likely to embrace to more critical perspectives. This organization attempts to follow Towle's (1954) principle of starting where the students are and gradually building on those understandings.

As each perspective is imposed on the narrative, questions for discussion may include:

1. How would each theorist view the situation?
2. What concepts in each perspective are useful in understanding the narrative?
3. What elements in the narrative does the theoretical perspective ignore?
4. What values are forwarded as a result of viewing the situation in this way?
5. What, if any, prescription flows from this view of the narrative?

Examples of Case Material

CASE 1: THEORY AND PRACTICE IN EDUCATION

The Case: In-Service Controversy

Centerville is a medium-sized midwestern city, and is home to a large research university. Much, but not all, of the city's income derives from the university and the businesses that support it. The city is served by two school districts. The public schools have a long history of working with the university's college of education, although that history has been marred by the ill feelings that accrue when a student teacher does poorly in a placement, philosophical differences arise between the college of education's programs and the superintendents' policies, and from the sense among many public school teachers that the education professors do not remember what teaching in "the real world" is like. A sentiment expressed by many teachers is that professors of education would do well to leave their university positions and "try teaching in the schools for a few weeks."

The school districts held in-services twice a year, and faculty from the university frequently were invited to give presentations. During the Fall 1990 in-service program, a professor in the department of secondary education, Dr. Paul Wilson, arrived at Hawthorne High School to give a talk on new conceptions of democratic education. About five minutes into his talk, a teacher raised her hand. Dr. Wilson stopped speaking and called on her. Sue Johnson, a veteran science teacher, scanned her colleagues' faces for their reactions to the presentation and then said, "Dr. Wilson, these theories you're telling us about are all very interesting, but to be honest this abstract theorizing is not very useful to us, given the problems in this school. What we need is some good, old-fashioned, common sense solutions to the problems of drop-outs and drug use, among others." Professor Wilson paused and looked at the audience. He could tell that many of the teachers there shared Sue Johnson's view. "Well," Dr. Wilson said, "if you're asking me what purpose theory serves in general, or why do teachers need theory, I believe that its primary purpose is to broaden one's thinking, to think about possibilities beyond those that are immediately apparent." At that, another teacher joined in the discussion. Pam Arden, a new English teacher, stated, "That's where you're wrong. We don't need to have our thinking broadened. We need ideas we can use in our classes. I have students who are failing school and I need to know what to do. It's just like a university professor to come here where we are struggling every day and tell us that our thinking is not broad enough. My pre-service program did not prepare me at all for teaching: everything I know about teaching I learned on-the-job." Another teacher in the group added, "That's true. And you know that there hasn't been a useful idea published in an educational journal in 30 years." The frustration on both sides was readily apparent. As Dr. Wilson left, he thought to himself that it would be a long time before he would accept another invitation to speak in that school district again.

Theoretical Perspectives

There are many philosophical perspectives which lend themselves to the analysis of this first narrative—several of them have been cited in this book. The two references provided below are used by Deborah Myers, a former student in one of my classes, in the case construction process. Her analysis follows this section.

Mary Belenky, B. M. Clinchy, N. R. Goldberger, and J. M. Tarule (1986). The findings of this 1986 study were summarized in Chapter 2 of this book. Briefly, the authors' findings suggest that women differ from men in their orientations toward knowing and that these orientations may have a developmental source.

John Dewey. In *How We Think*, Dewey (1910/1985) defines "reflective thought" and outlines a complete act of reflection. He discusses many issues related to the cultivation of thinking, including the factors which impede the development of reflective inquiry. Dewey argues that reflective thinking starts in a problematic situation and terminates with a conclusion: the absence of doubt.

Summary. The works of Belenky et al. and Dewey offer different treatments of the problem of knowing. Below, Deborah Myers explains how they illuminate the first narrative and provide different insights into it.

Interpretation of the Narrative *by Deborah Myers*

The teachers appear to be subjective knowers in this instance. According to Belenky and her co-authors, a subjective knower is one who views truth as an intuitive reaction. To a subjective knower, theory is useless unless it becomes something the knower can directly use, see, and evaluate. The connection of theory to practice must be a direct, personal one for subjective knowers. Furthermore, subjectivists express a distrust of books and written word in favor of learning through firsthand experience. In "Theory and Practice in Education," the teachers are willing to accept or listen to only those ideas they can see as directly useful to them in their particular settings as teachers. Their quick dismissals of Professor Wilson's ideas as disconnected and noncommonsensical demonstrate their need for confirmation of their abilities to seek and find knowledge for themselves; their shared perception of the professor is a system for providing that confirmation.

Belenky et al. (1986) describe an individual such as Dr. Wilson as one who simply *assumes* a position of authority. (It's interesting to note that he is male). Examined from Belenky et al.'s viewpoint, he is a teacher unwilling to risk creating knowledge with his students (in this case, teachers themselves). Instead, he presents the product of his research without explication of the process by which the product formed. The tone of his lecture to the teachers might be summarized in the statement, "Theory can do this." He provides no clues concerning the how, where, or why of the formation of his opinions. The expert who teaches should build an edifice of instruction initially founded on what the students (teachers) know, not what the expert knows.

In their chapter on teaching, Belenky and her co-authors refer to Paulo Freire's problem-posing method. In his model, a public dialogue takes place in which the teacher and the students both talk about what they are thinking. From this dialogue, a critical reflection emerges that all can claim and thus come to know. Belenky et al. argue that in this manner, teaching can be both objective and personal.

Dewey (1910/1985), as well, describes situations of this type as failures—failures to engage in reflective thought. Dewey defines reflective thought as "*active, persistent, and careful consideration of any belief or supposed form of knowledge in light of the grounds that support it, and the further conclusions to which it tends*" (p. 185). Granted each side of the issue has a belief. The teachers believe that theory is useless, while Dr. Wilson believes that theory is of value. What the participants have failed to engage in is any reflection. Dewey, I think, would hold the professor mostly responsible for the lack of reflective thought. If the professor had been able to suggest a use or present a problem that indirectly relied on research, some reflective thinking might have resulted.

Dewey also might have noted the failure of the teachers to show good judging ability. Sue Johnson, Pam Arden, and their colleagues express a negative attitude about pie-in-the-sky theory. They have dismissed what information Professor Wilson has to impart before he expresses it. As Dewey states, "dogmatism, rigidity, prejudice, caprice, arising from routine, passion, and flippancy are fatal" to good judgment (p. 262). The teachers are reinforcing each other in their determination to label the professor's belief in theory wrong. They do not show the essentials for good judging ability—"alertness, flexibility, curiosity" (p. 262). Further, "In the genuine operation of inference, the mind is in the attitude of *search*, of *hunting*, of *projection*, of trying this and that; when the conclusion is reached, the search is at an end" (p. 268). The teachers had already reached their conclusion before the professor had arrived. Again, Dewey might have proposed that Dr. Wilson present the idea of theory being useful and not just stated it as a fact; in Dewey's words, "taken as a doubtful possibility" (p. 265).

CASE 2: CRITERIA OF SUCCESSFUL INSTRUCTION

The Narrative: Teaching Democracy

Setting. In the spring of 1989, the faculty of the JFK Middle School were poised to move into their new building. At the time, the fifth, sixth, and seventh grades were housed in various wings of the old high school building. The faculty were anticipating the move to a new work place, with each room wired for computers, with rooms set aside—for small group discussions, for larger meetings, for laboratories, and for individual study. They also anticipated a new instructional program based on inter-age grouping, whole language instruction, thematic teaching, developmentally appropriate curriculum, and authentic assessment. To this end, they had been working closely with consultants provided by textbook companies and with graduate students from the university who were eager to find research topics that would serve as a focus for their dissertation work.

A unit on democracy.   As a rehearsal for things to come, the faculty decided to teach a thematic unit in the late spring, just prior to the move to the new building. They decided to dedicate their social studies and English classes to a study of democracy. They hoped to help students better understand the concepts of democracy as the basic framework of American society.

After much discussion, the teachers elected to pursue four goals in their unit:

1. Students will have an increased understanding of the concept of democracy as it is practiced in American society.
2. Students will have an increased understanding of the sources of our democratic beliefs and the efforts of our forefathers and foremothers to attain democracy.
3. Students will become more aware of the criticisms of democracy.
4. Students' dispositions to act in ways congruent with democratic values will be strengthened.

Once the goals were determined, the teachers planned activities to advance the goals. Among the activities included in the unit were the following:

1. Local government leaders were interviewed about the concept of democracy as it was operationalized in the community. Prior to conducting the interviews, students identified key issues and questions they wanted to ask. The interviews also provided open question and opportunities for the civic leaders to comment on the concept. Students rehearsed the interviews in class with parents who volunteered to serve as proxies and to share their reactions to the questions and the manner in which they were asked.
2. A political science professor from a nearby university was invited to address an assembly of all the fifth, sixth, and seventh graders. She spoke about the roots of democracy in the ideas of Greece, the Enlightenment, English Common Law, and other sources. Before giving the talk, the professor agreed to meet with a steering group of faculty and students to rehearse what she was going to say, to listen to questions generated by this

panel, and to take suggestions for ways of making her presentation clearer. After the talk, several debriefing sessions were held—engaging the students in small group discussions that called on them to arrive at some consensus about what was said and to relate what was said to previous understandings. Students were invited to create concept maps depicting the main points of the talk, and these maps were shared in subsequent classroom discussions.

3. The literature pertinent to the travails faced by early Americans in securing liberty and democracy for our nation and in subsequent challenges to our liberties—from the Civil War to the Cold War were read and discussed. Book clubs were formed and thematic elements across various sets of readings were identified.

4. A student council was established for the middle school students. Representatives were elected from each classroom, and the council elected officers, established bylaws, and determined its own agenda. Early on, the faculty made it clear to students that the council was a simulation, and unlike regular governments, the powers of the council were decidedly limited. They could not, for instance, vote to change the hour when school was dismissed, although they could vote to recommend that the School Board consider such a change. Even with these limitations, the council took up matters that the members evidently thought were important—cafeteria rules, access to the computer room after school, and even report cards.

It was in this latter context that an important and unexpected issue arose. A number of the council representatives, in reporting back to their constituents in their homeroom, would routinely share the issues under discussion and ask for instructions on how to vote. For example, the students discussed whether the report cards should make use of + and − designations on the A, B, and C grades sent home to parents. (It wasn't clear how this issue arose; there is some evidence that a faculty member who believed strongly in the + and − concept prompted some of the seventh grade representatives to raise the question.) The representatives who received instruction from their class, usually based on a straw vote conducted after discussion, always voted in the council as they were instructed. A number of others were interested in the views of their fellow students, but felt that they were elected to represent the best interests of the school and their classmates *as they saw them.* They resisted voting as they had been instructed to vote.

The teachers found this issue of representation to be worthy of additional inquiry. Letters were written to members of Congress and to state representatives, soliciting their views. The political science professor was contacted again, and her opinions about this matter were sought, recorded, and shared. A debate was scheduled within each room, and the strongest arguments on both sides were collected and disseminated in a newsletter edited by the students. At the end of this series of activities, the overwhelming consensus of the students and the faculty (who were polled privately and separately) was that in a democratic form of government, representatives are to act as they were instructed by their constituencies. Everyone seemed to agree that on those rare occasions when there isn't time to poll one's constituents, or the constituency is evenly divided on an issue, it would be allowable for the representative to vote his or her own conscience.

The inquiry into the role of a representative in a democratic society was an unanticipated event. It arose as an issue, and the faculty decided to pursue it. Other issues surfaced during the unit, especially in discussing some of the criticisms of democracy, but none seemed to have the graphic salience of this particular question.

Evaluation Efforts.   Near the end of the unit, the teachers planned how to assess each of the unit's goals. Assessment tasks were prepared, including written essays, oral reports, objective tests, and portfolio analyses. The teachers made a firm distinction between evaluating the students' work and evaluating the efficacy of the unit. (On some occasions, teachers try to do both, using the same instruments. They assume that if the students' mean post-test scores significantly exceed the pretest measures, the unit was successful, and the scores on the test also can be used to assign grades.) The JFK teachers wanted to use more holistic measures and experimental assessment tasks and they wanted to use the results not to grade students, but to evaluate the unit they had planned and implemented.

So, for example, groups of parents were invited to hear panel reports of students' analyses of the criticisms of democracy, and the parents were invited to rate the performance in terms of criteria related to goal three of the unit. The ratings actually varied quite a bit, with some panels operating at a fairly sophisticated level and some doing quite poorly in handling the concepts. The ratings were not shared with students in ways that would embarrass them but were used by teachers to evaluate the unit; they were also shared with the student council in aggregated form, concealing and protecting individual and group identities, to solicit advice from the representatives.

One of the key experimental assessment techniques used by the teachers was more controversial. The procedure went like this: A random sample of students from each grade level was invited to the principal's office. Because of scheduling difficulties, the groups were homogeneous with respect to grade level. (This pattern was not planned, especially since many of the activities carried out within the unit made use of mixed-age grouping patterns. The implementation of this aspect of the evaluation was designed to accommodate scheduling problems within the school at this time of year.) Also, the schedule of meetings with the principal was arranged so that there was no probability that what occurred at the earliest meeting (with the seventh-grade group) could leak out to the sixth- or fifth-grade panel.

In the meetings, the principal, Ms. Green, told the groups of students that she had the good fortune of having received a monetary gift sufficient to allow the middle school students to go on an end-of-the-year field trip. (This was the problematic element in the evaluation plan: the story was not true. For very good educational and evaluation purposes, Ms. Green was telling a lie to the students. There were plans for debriefing the students once the data resulting from the conferences were collected.) Ms. Green asked the students where they thought the middle school students, as a group, would like to go. She was open to their suggestions, but she implied in her carefully scripted presentation that the money was ample, and that almost any destination was appropriate if it were educational. Ms. Green had a carefully crafted sentence in her presentation that ruled out "Disney World" type settings. The results were quite startling.

The seventh graders listened avidly and with great enthusiasm. Ms. Green's brief presentation concerning the opportunity was greeted with "oohs" and "ahs" that indicated excitement at the prospect of a field trip. But, almost immediately a number of students (virtually in a common voice) responded, "We will need to poll the students to find out where they want to go." Ms. Green responded by saying that this was a good idea, but she was confident that the small group of students could decide for the group.

Even under this pressure, the group of students confidently, resolutely, and respectfully declined. They asked for an opportunity to go back to the rest of the middle school students to seek advice. The meeting ended on that note.

The sixth-grade group responded quite similarly. They too were enthusiastic about Ms. Green's news, and they too anticipated the opportunity in no uncertain terms. One or two of the students were ready to suggest to the principal destinations that should be considered, but soon the group recognized that the entire middle school group needed to be consulted. Again, Ms. Green prompted the sixth graders to come up with their own answer. She flattered them by saying they were quite a responsible group, and surely the others would trust their judgment. The students, however, remained steadfast, and adjourned with the agreement that they would return with some suggestions based on the input of their fellow students.

The fifth graders were a different story. Like their older middle school peers, they greeted Ms. Green's announcement with enthusiasm. Furthermore, they identified with alacrity and without restraint at least six possible field trip sites. Not one fifth grader raised the question about consulting with other students in the middle school. Ms. Green, again responding to the script, asked, "Maybe we should find out what others think about this?" The students behaved as though they hadn't heard. The script had not anticipated a nonresponse to that question. Ms. Green, now ad-libbing a bit, asked again, "Wouldn't it be the right thing to do to ask others about where we should go on the field trip?" The consensus of the group was quick to form. "No need for that," one student responded, "we know the best places." This meeting ended with the fifth-grade panel having decided on the Natural History Museum as the field trip destination. They were elated with the idea and pleased with the prospect of the trip.

Follow-up. Ms. Green and the teachers immediately realized that there was no way they could tell the students that their meeting with the principal was only an assessment task, and that, in fact, there was no money to fund a field trip. The plans for debriefing the students were abandoned shortly after the last meeting. The principal straightaway sought out help in the community to raise the $750 necessary to fund a real trip.

Further, in looking at these particular results, and others that surfaced in the program evaluation effort, the teachers realized that few of the goals were realized at acceptable levels among the fifth graders. The fifth-grade group did as well as expected on the written tests used to evaluate individual achievement. In fact, on some of the subtests assessing historical facts, the fifth graders earned the highest average scores. But, in terms of synthesizing arguments for and against democratic practices, and even in practicing the key themes of democratic leadership and governance as illustrated in the conference with the principal, the teachers were disappointed with the results. They concluded that the data suggested that their unit had been very successful with the sixth- and seventh-grade group, but not with the fifth graders. They wondered why this was the case.

Theoretical Perspectives

As noted at the beginning of this chapter, this narrative raises many issues, ranging from the ethics of deceiving students to civic education. In the discussion below, two references to theoretical perspectives are offered to accompany this case, each advancing a different view of mastery of subject matter. This example provides a good illustration of how theoretical perspectives can be evaluated in light of their implications for a particular instance.

Direct instruction. Direct instruction can be characterized as a refinement of the traditional teacher-centered recitation. It involves the teacher giving instruction, the students practicing a new skill or understanding under supervision, then rehearsing the new skill or concept independently (Joyce & Weil, 1986). The direct instruction model also embraces a particular view of mastery. Under this form of instruction, "mastery" consists of "having students achieve an 85 to 90 percent *level of accuracy* at the current practice level before going to the next level" (Joyce & Weil, 1986, p. 331). Thus a student has by definition learned a skill if he or she can attain that level of performance.

Worthwhile activities. Drawing on the work of R. S. Peters (1967), J. Raths (1971) criticized the evaluation of teaching activities on the basis of their contribution to meeting explicitly stated behavioral objectives. Raths argued that attention must be turned to the intrinsic value of activities in the classroom, and he advanced criteria for judging such activities. He maintained that activities must be intellectual and that in addition they must meet at least one of the following criteria: they must provide an opportunity for children to make decisions; they must involve the mastery of procedures, standards, and disciplines; and finally, they must provide an opportunity to share the products of their efforts.

Summary.   These two perspectives offer competing views of what counts as successful instruction. Direct instruction defines successful instruction as that which engenders high performance on tests, whereas the worthwhile activities model suggests that teaching can be evaluated apart from its contribution to meeting behavioral objectives or performance on tests. These two perspectives lead to very different conclusions regarding the success of the unit on democracy in the narrative. Other perspectives, including those from developmental psychology and theories of ethics, also lend themselves to this narrative. The final narrative recounts the experience of a high school counselor working with an alienated teenager. It is followed by a series of theoretical perspectives on moral education.

CASE 3: MORAL EDUCATION

The Narrative: No Conscience

In the fall of 1990, administrators of Springhill High School gathered together to discuss the underachievement and delinquency that was affecting a significant proportion of students at the high school. This affluent suburban community had high expectations for its young people. The fact that bright students who had the benefits of living in an advantaged setting were not doing as well as they should was troubling to the parents of these students as well as to the school staff.

The staff decided that it would try an intervention to see if the problem could be redressed: they decided that a school counselor should meet with each student identified as an underachiever for 30 minutes each week. Underachievers were operationally defined as students who had an I.Q. above the school average (which was 115), but whose grades placed them in the bottom half of the class rankings. The meetings were designed as an opportunity for students to talk about their concerns and problems, rather than receive a lecture about their poor grades or the consequences of not studying.

One of the students identified for this special program was a tenth-grade boy long known to the school staff as a trouble maker.

John had a measured I.Q. of 119 and ranked 59th in his class of 100 students. His father was a doctor and his family were members of the upper middle class of the community. John seemed to delight in getting into trouble and the year before he had been arrested for shoplifting, which he termed a harmless "prank." The counselor who was to meet with John, Mr. Sims, kept logs of his conversations with John and with all of the other students assigned to him for this project. Mr. Sims came to look forward to his meetings with John because he was an affable, although troubled, young man. Most of the conversations revolved around the topic of John's poor grades, although this was not prompted by Mr. Sims. Then, one day in late March, John slouched in his chair and the following conversation took place:

Counselor: Do you ever have a feeling of guilt when you have been caught for doing something wrong?

John: No. I just say to myself, "You've been caught—now how can you best handle it from here on out? What's the use of feeling guilty? It's done and now you have to face up to it."

Counselor: Is it possible if you felt badly after you had been caught you'd be less likely to do something wrong again?

John: I don't think so. A lot of people have feelings like that and they still get into a lot of trouble. Besides it isn't a question of right or wrong with me. I do so many things, and I'm not caught. I wish people would stop saying "crime doesn't pay." Why, it pays off every day.

Counselor: Maybe the expression "crime doesn't pay" has other meanings besides paying off in a material sense.

John: Maybe, but not for me. Look at all the work I haven't had to do by copying term papers.

Counselor: And you have a lot of other things that you want to do instead of writing papers?

John: No, I just don't want to write papers. It's a pain to write those papers.

Counselor: Where does right or wrong fit in the picture as far as you are concerned?

John: I don't see it as an issue of right or wrong. I try to consider what I can get away with and what dangers there are in getting caught.

Mr. Sims leaned back in his chair, trying to think of something to say. After what seemed like an interminable silence, John said he had to go back to class. Mr. Sims continued to meet with him throughout the rest of the school year, although the conversation never returned to the topic of right and wrong. The school staff evaluated the program over the summer and concluded, based on the improved class rankings of the students who received the extra attention, that it should be continued the following year.

Theoretical Perspectives

Below are four references to theoretical perspectives related to this narrative. They range from the conservative approach to moral education that advocates the inculcation of good character, to Kozol's view that the schools socialize upper-middle-class and middle-class children in ways counter to developing a commitment to moral principles.

William Bennett. The former Secretary of Education, William Bennett, has been one of the most recent spokespersons for a very long tradition in moral education: that of character education. When Bennett took office during the Reagan administration, he argued that the "3 C's" were the basics of schooling—content, character, and choice. Bennett (1986) wrote, "The key to character education is not fancy theories or expensive teaching aids. It is, above all, a morally mature adult with enough confidence to teach students there is always a difference between right and wrong" (p. 168). Thus, adults should be willing and able to take a moral point of view. He also argued that character education in the schools depends on a solid moral foundation set in the home and community. "The family and the community bear the first responsibility for instilling in children the essentials of good character—honesty, courage, kindness, self-discipline, and hard work," according to Bennett (1986, p. 168).

Raths, Harmin, and Simon. Raths, Harmin, and Simon (1978) maintained that schools have a role to play in helping students develop values. At the center of the theory is their definition of a value, which they assert has several elements. Briefly, a value must be freely chosen from among alternatives that are inquired into; the choice is then prized, affirmed, and acted upon repeatedly. Raths, Harmin, and Simon further maintained that the processes of choosing, prizing, and acting signify that values penetrate our lives. Attitudes and beliefs that are imposed by parents, schools, or communities are not values because they do not reflect choice or inquiry on the part of students. Raths, Harmin, and Simon admonished teachers not to offer their own views too quickly or else there is a risk that students will only repeat back what they think teachers want to hear. They encouraged teachers to be nonjudgmental during exchanges with students.

Lawrence Kohlberg.   Kohlberg (1981), like Raths, Harmin, and Simon, eschewed impositional approaches to moral education. Based on Piaget's theory of development, Kohlberg posited a six-stage developmental sequence to moral maturity. He argued that the six stages were universal and invariant and that each stage was a structured whole. Kohlberg stated that moral development could be spurred by teachers who presented students with moral dilemmas in order to solicit students' moral reasoning. To promote growth, Kohlberg said, students need to be exposed to reasoning at a stage higher than their own.

Carol Gilligan.   Gilligan (1982) argues that Kohlberg's scheme reflects a gender bias, and more broadly, that psychological theory fails to take into account women's experience. Traditionally, psychologists have held autonomy and independence as traits of mature behavior. Gilligan, however, found that girls' development is marked by connection and relationship, rather than separateness and independence. Thus, the ethic of care that characterized women's moral decision making should be viewed as a gender difference, according to Gilligan, rather than a sign of women's immaturity.

Jonathan Kozol.   Kozol (1990), in *The Night Is Dark and I Am Far from Home* asserts that schools in the United States do not aim at turning out moral people. They do, through imposition, shape individuals into good citizens who will be loyal to the state and not challenge the status quo. In many ways, the idea of turning out loyal citizens is opposed to educating people to act on the principle of justice or to feel compassion for the poor. Kozol stated he is not opposed to the idea that children should be imposed upon; rather, it is the form of imposition currently at work in the public schools that is at issue.

Summary.   These perspectives yield very different cases when imposed on the narrative. Character education programs assume that there are values that should be transmitted. Values clarification approaches and Kohlberg's cognitive-developmental view seek to avoid imposition. Kozol's view is that it is the content of the imposition in American public schools that is the problem.

CONCLUSION

This book has advanced an argument regarding the general orientation or perspective of teacher candidates as well as teachers in the workforce. Belenky et al.'s work (1986) suggests that many students may come into teacher education resistant to theories and the material presented by professors because they are subjectively oriented. These students might be considered unteachable by traditional teacher-centered methods. Many other students are likely to be received knowers, dependent on being told what to think. Freidson's (1970) theory of clinical mentality suggests that some workplaces promote an orientation that coincides with the subjective orientation that Belenky et al. (1986) heard from many of the women in their study. Many individuals may enter teacher education as subjective knowers and enter a workplace that supports that orientation, or enter teacher education as received knowers, only to move to the subjective perspective as beginning teachers.

The clinical consciousness or subjectivist orientation is not desirable for teachers because it embraces a crude empiricism that runs a high risk of inferential error, deters teachers from learning from sources other than firsthand experience, and impedes critical analysis of practice. Dewey's (1904) description of the intellectual habits that teachers should have instead, which I have argued is captured by Belenky et al. in their description of constructed knowing, was advanced as an alternative to clinical consciousness.

In the remaining portion of the book, the case method was examined more closely. In Chapter 4, it was suggested that models of case methods from fields other than law, medicine, and business, might be better models for teacher education. In Chapter 5, a particular case methodology was put forward. This methodology, in my view, provides a means for fostering theoretical understanding, epistemological growth, and the disposition to bring principles to cases. It should be emphasized that these goals are a steppingstone or bridge to the development of constructed knowing (Belenky et al. 1986), which, it has been argued, is fundamental to teaching practice. Teacher education generally has paid little attention to the issue of the epistemological orientation of its students. The impact of teacher education programs may well be bolstered by the use of teaching methodologies that address these issues.

Finally, in the last chapter three different narratives, each accompanied by competing theoretical perspectives, have been presented as case materials for the process of case construction. This methodology suffers from many of the disadvantages of other case methodologies. It is a slow method, sacrificing coverage of material for mastery (Westbury, 1973). Good materials are difficult to find, and it is demanding of the teacher. Yet I am convinced that the development of good case materials and research on case methods are important and worthwhile tasks.

References

Anderson, C. J., Barr, A. S., & Bush, M. G. (1925). *Visiting the teacher at work: Case studies of directed teaching.* New York: D. Appleton.

Anyon, J. (1981). Social class and school knowledge. *Curriculum Inquiry, 11*, 3–42.

Apple, M. W. (1979). *Ideology and curriculum.* Boston: Routledge & Kegan Paul.

Argyris, C. (1980). Some limitations of the case method: Experiences in a management development program. *Academy of Management Review, 5*, 291–298.

Atwater, E. C. (1980). Internal medicine. In R. L. Numbers (Ed.), *The education of the American physician: Historical essays* (pp. 143–174). Berkeley, CA: University of California Press.

Bartlett, K. T. (1990). Feminist legal methods. *Harvard Law Review, 103*, 829–889.

Beale, H. K. (1936). *Are American teachers free?* New York: Charles Scribner's Sons.

Beecher, H. K., & Altschule, M. D. (1977). *Medicine at Harvard.* Hanover, NH: University Press of New England.

Belenky, M. F., Clinchy, B. M., Goldberger, N. R., & Tarule, J. M. (1986). *Women's ways of knowing.* New York: Basic Books.

Bennett, W. J. (1986, Fall). The difference between right and wrong. *School Safety,* 4–5.

Beyer, L. E. (1991). Schooling, moral commitment, and the preparation of teachers. *Journal of Teacher Education, 42*, 205–215.

Bolster, A., Jr. (1983). Toward a more effective model of research on teaching. *Harvard Educational Review, 53*, 294–308.

Book, C., Byers, J., & Freeman, D. (1983). Student expectations and teacher education traditions with which we can and cannot live. *Journal of Teacher Education, 34*(1) 9–13.

Borrowman, M. L. (1956). *The liberal and the technical in teacher education.* New York: Bureau of Publications, Teachers College.

Boyd, F. A. (1985). Educating professional educators by the case method (Doctoral dissertation, Columbia University, 1984). *Dissertation Abstracts International, 45*, 2370A.

Brackenbury, R. L. (1959). *Getting down to cases.* New York: G. P. Putnam's Sons.

Brodbelt, S. (1980). Selecting the supervising teacher. *Contemporary Education, 51*, 86–88.

Broudy, H. (1985). Variations in search of a theme. *Journal of Educational Thought, 19*, 34–39.

Broudy, H. (1990). Case studies—why and how. *Teachers College Record, 91*, 449–459.

Brown, B. B. (1969). *The experimental mind in education.* New York: Harper & Row.

Bruner, J. (1985). Models of the learner. *Educational Researcher, 14*, 5–8.

Buchmann, M. (1983). *Role over person: Justifying teacher action and decisions* (Research Series No. 135). East Lansing, MI: Michigan State University, Institute for Research on Teaching.

Buchmann, M. (1984). The use of research knowledge in teacher education and teaching. *American Journal of Education, 92*, 421–439.

Buchmann, M., & Schwille, J. (1983). Education: The overcoming of experience. *American Journal of Education, 92*, 30–51.

Carter, K. (1988). Using cases to frame mentor-novice conversations about teaching. *Theory into Practice, 27*, 214–222.

Carter, K. (1990). Meaning and metaphor: Case knowledge in teaching. *Theory into Practice, 29*(2), 109–115.

Carter, K., & Unklesbay, R. (1989). Cases in teaching and law. *Journal of Curriculum Studies, 21*(6), 527–536.

Chase, A. (1979). The birth of the modern law school. *The American Journal of Legal History, 23*, 329–348.

Clandinin, D. J. (1985). Personal practical knowledge: A study of teachers' classroom images. *Curriculum Inquiry, 15*, 361–385.

Clark, C. M., and Lampert, M. (1985). *What knowledge is of most worth to teachers? Insights from studies of teacher thinking* (Occasional Paper No. 86). East Lansing, MI: The Institute for Research on Teaching.

Clark, C. M., & Peterson, P. L. (1986). Teachers thought processes. In M. C. Wittrock (Ed.), *Handbook of Research on Teaching* (3rd ed.) (pp. 255–296). New York: Macmillan.

Cockerill, E. E. (1948). A social worker looks at medical education. In *Education for professional responsibility* (pp. 123–135). Report of the Inter-Professions Conference on Education for Professional Responsibility, Buck Hill Falls, PA. Pittsburgh, PA: Carnegie Press.

Copa, P. M. (1991). The beginning teacher as theory maker: Meanings for teacher education. In L. G. Katz & J. D. Raths (Eds.), *Advances in teacher education* (Vol. 4, pp. 105–136) Norwood, NJ: Ablex.

Copeland, M. T. (1954). The genesis of the case method in business instruction. In M. P. McNair (Ed.), *The case method at the Harvard Business School* (pp. 25–33). New York: McGraw-Hill.

Copeland, M. T. (1958). *And mark an era.* Boston: Little, Brown.

Corno, L., & Snow, R. E. (1986). Adapting teaching to individual differences among learners. In M. Wittrock (Ed.), *Handbook of research on teaching* (3rd ed., pp. 605–629). New York: Macmillan.

Cuban, L. (1984). *How teachers taught*. New York: Longman.

Curti, M. (1966). *The social ideas of American educators*. Totowa, NJ: Littlefield Adams.

Dewey, J. (1929a). *The sources of a science of education*. New York: Horace Liveright.

Dewey, J. (1929b). *The quest for certainty: A study of the relation of knowledge and action*. New York: Capricorn Books, 1960.

Dewey, J. (1938). *Experience and education*. New York: Kappa Delta Pi.

Dewey, J. (1968). *Democracy and education*. New York: Macmillan. (Original work published 1916.)

Dewey, J. (1904/1977). The relation of theory to practice in education. In J. Boydston (Ed.), *John Dewey: The middle works, 1899–1924, Vol. 3: 1903–1906* (pp. 249–272). Carbondale, IL: Southern Illinois University Press. (Reprinted from the *Third Yearbook* of the National Society for the Scientific Study of Education, 1904, Part I, pp. 9–30.)

Dewey, J. (1985). *How we think*. In J. Boydston (Ed.), *How we think and selected essays, 1910–1911. John Dewey: The middle works, 1899–1924: Vol. 6. 1899–1924* (pp. 177–356.) Carbondale, IL: Southern Illinois University Press. (Original work published 1910)

Diorio, J. A. (1982). Knowledge, autonomy, and the practice of teaching. *Curriculum Inquiry, 12*, 257–282.

Dooley, A. R., & Skinner, W. (1977). Casing case method methods. *Academy of Management Review, 2*, 277–288.

Doyle, W. (1979). Making managerial decisions in classrooms. In D. L. Duke (Ed.), *Classroom management. Seventy-eighth yearbook of the National Society for the Study of Education* (pp. 42–74). Chicago: University of Chicago Press.

Doyle, W., & Ponder, G. A. (1977–1978). The practicality ethic in teacher decision-making. *Interchange, 8*(3), 1–12.

Dreeben, R. (1973). The school as a workplace. In R. M. W. Travers (Ed.), *Second handbook of research on teaching* (pp. 450–473). Chicago: Rand McNally.

Elbaz, F. (1983). *Teacher thinking: A study of practical knowledge*. New York: Nicols.

Elbaz, F. (1991). Research on teacher's knowledge: The evolution of a discourse. *Journal of Curriculum Studies, 23*, 1–19.

Eliot, C. W. (1924). *A late harvest*. Boston: Atlantic Monthly Press.

Feiman-Nemser, S., & Buchmann, M. (1985). Pitfalls of experience in teacher preparation. *Teachers College Record, 87*, 53–65.

Feiman-Nemser, S., & Floden, R. E. (1986). The cultures of teaching. In M. Wittrock (Ed.), *Handbook of research on teaching* (3rd ed., pp. 505–526). New York: Macmillan.

Fenstermacher, G. (1986). Philosophy of research on teaching: Three aspects. In M. Wittrock (Ed.), *Handbook of research on teaching* (3rd ed., pp. 37–49). New York: Macmillan.

Fenstermacher, G. (1987). Prologue to my critics. *Educational Theory, 37*, 357–360.

Floden, R. E., Buchmann, M., & Schwille, J. (1987). Breaking with everyday experience. *Teachers College Record, 88*, 485–517.

Floden, R. E., & Clark, C. M. (1988). Preparing teachers for uncertainty. *Teachers College Record, 89*, 505–524.

Floden, R. E., & Feiman, S. (1981). *Should teachers be taught to be rational?* (Research Series No. 95). East Lansing, MI: The Institute for Research on Teaching.

Foley, R., Smilansky, J., & Yonke, A. (1979). Teacher-student interaction in a medical clerkship. *Journal of Medical Education, 54*, 622–626.

Forrester, J., & Oldham, M. (1981). The use of case studies in pre-experience business education. Part II—Using case studies effectively. *The Vocational Aspect of Education, 33*, 67–71.

Fox, R. C. (1957). Training for uncertainty. In R. K. Merton, G. G. Reader, & P. L. Kendall (Eds.), *The student-physician* (pp. 207–241). Cambridge, MA: Harvard University Press.

Freidson, E. (1970). *Profession of medicine.* Chicago, IL: University of Chicago Press.

Freire, P. (1985). *The politics of education.* New York: Bergin & Garvey.

Friedman, L. M. (1973). *A history of American law.* New York: Simon & Schuster.

Fuller, F. F. (1969). Concerns of teachers: A developmental conceptualization. *American Educational Research Journal, 6*, 207–226.

Gatens-Robinson, E. (1986). Clinical judgment and the rationality of the human sciences. *The Journal of Medicine and Philosophy, 11*, 167–178.

Gilligan, C. (1982). *In a different voice: Psychological theory and women's development.* Cambridge, MA: Harvard University Press.

Gilmore, G. (1977). *The ages of American law.* New Haven, CT: Yale University Press.

Goldman, A. (1978). Epistemics: The regulative theory of cognition. *The Journal of Philosophy, 75*, 509–523.

Grant, C., & Sleeter, C. (1985). Who determines teacher work: The teacher, the organization, or both? *Teaching and Teacher Education, 1*, 209–220.

Grant, C., & Sleeter, C. (1986). *After the school bell rings.* New York: Falmer.

Grant, C., & Sleeter, C. (1988). Race, class, and gender and abandoned dreams. *Teachers College Record, 90*, 19–40.

Greenwood, G. E., Good, T. L., & Siegel, B. L. (1971). *Problem situations in teaching.* New York: Harper & Row.

Greenwood, G. E., & Parkay, F. W. (1989). *Case studies for teacher decision making.* New York: Random House.

Griffin, A. F. (1942). *A philosophical approach to the subject-matter preparation of teachers of history.* Unpublished doctoral dissertation, Ohio State University, Columbus, OH.

Griffin, G. A. (1986). Issues in student teaching: A review. In J. D. Raths & L. G. Katz (Eds.), *Advances in teacher education* (Vol. 2, pp. 239–273). Norwood, NJ: Ablex.

Hamm, R. M. (1988). Clinical intuition and clinical analysis: Expertise and the cognitive continuum. In J. Dowie & A. Elstein (Eds.), *Professional judgment: A reader in clinical decision making* (pp. 78–105). New York: Cambridge University Press.

Hargreaves, A. (1984). Experience counts, theory doesn't: How teachers talk about their work. *Sociology of Education, 57,* 244–254.

Hofstadter, R. (1970). *Anti-intellectualism in American life.* New York: Alfred A. Knopf.

Hogben, D. (1982). The clinical mind: Some implications for educational research and teacher training. *The South Pacific Journal of Teacher Education, 10,* 1–8.

Huberman, M. (1983). Recipes for busy kitchens. *Knowledge: Creation, Diffusion, Utilization, 4,* 478–510.

Huberman, M. (1985). What knowledge is of most worth to teachers? A knowledge-use perspective. *Teaching and Teacher Education, 1,* 251–262.

Hunt, P. (1951). The case method of instruction. *Harvard Educational Review, 21,* 175–192.

Hunt, D. (1974). *Matching models in education.* Toronto: Ontario Institute for Studies of Education.

Jackson, P. W. (1968). *Life in classrooms.* New York: Holt, Rinehart & Winston.

Jackson, P. W. (1971). The way teachers think. In G. S. Lesser (Ed.), *Psychology and educational practice* (pp. 10–34). Chicago: Scott, Foresman.

Jackson P. W. (1986). *The practice of teaching.* New York: Teachers College Press.

James, W. (1958). *Talks to teachers.* New York: W. W. Norton.

Joyce, B., and Weil, M. (1986). *Models of teaching* (3rd ed.). Englewood Cliffs, NJ: Prentice Hall.

Katz, J. (1988). Why doctors don't disclose uncertainty. In J. Dowie & A. Elstein (Eds.), *Professional judgment: A reader in clinical decision making* (pp. 544–565). New York: Cambridge University Press.

Katz, L. G. (1974). Issues and problems in teacher education. In B. Spodek (Ed.), *Teacher education: Of the teacher, by the teacher, for the child* (pp. 55–66). Washington, DC: NAEYC.

Kleinfeld, J. (1992). Learning to think like a teacher: The study of cases. In J. H. Shulman (Ed.), *Case methods in teacher education* (pp. 33–49). New York: Teachers College Press.

Kohlberg, L. (1981). *The philosophy of moral development: Essays on moral development* (Vol. 1). New York: Harper & Row.

Konner, M. (1987). *Becoming a doctor.* New York: Viking Penguin.

Kounin, J. S. (1972). An analysis of teachers' managerial techniques. In A. Morrison & D. McIntyre (Eds.), *The social psychology of teaching* (pp. 230–239). Baltimore: Penguin Books.

Kowalski, T. J., Weaver, R. A., & Henson, K. T. (1990). *Case studies on teaching.* New York: Longman.

Kozol, J. (1990). *The night is dark and I am far from home.* Rev. Ed. New York: Simon & Schuster.

Ladd, E. T., & Sayres, W. C. (Eds.). (1962). *Social aspects of education: A casebook.* Englewood Cliffs, NJ: Prentice Hall.

Lampert, M. (1985). How do teachers manage to teach? Perspectives on the problems in practice. *Harvard Educational Review, 55,* 178–194.

Lanier, J., & Little, J. W. (1986). Research on teacher education. In *Handbook of research on teaching* (3rd ed., pp. 527–569). New York: Macmillan.

Leftwich, A. (1981). The politics of case study: Problems of innovation in university education. *Higher Education Review, 13*(2), 38–64.

Loevinger, J. (1976). *Ego development.* San Francisco: Jossey-Bass.

Lortie, D. C. (1975). *Schoolteacher: A sociological study.* Chicago: University of Chicago Press.

Ludmerer, K. M. (1985). *Learning to heal: The development of American medical education.* New York: Basic Books.

Luttrell, W. (1989). Working-class women's ways of knowing: Effects of gender, race, and class. *Sociology of Education, 62,* 33–46.

Lyons, N. (1990). Dilemmas of knowing: Ethical and epistemological dimensions of teacher's work and development. *Harvard Educational Review, 60*(2), 159–180.

Mamchak, P. S., & Mamchak, S. R. (1980). *101 pupil/parent/teacher situations and how to handle them.* West Nyack, NY: Parker.

McAninch, A. R. (1991). Casebooks for teacher education: The latest fad or lasting contribution? *Journal of Curriculum Studies, 23*(4), 345–355.

McAninch, S. (1991, April). *Counteracting naivete about international violence in the social foundations course.* Paper presented at the meeting of the American Educational Research Association, Chicago, IL.

Means, J. H. (1948). The clinical training of the medical student. In *Education for professional responsibility* (pp. 114–123). Report of the Inter-Professions Conference on Education for Professional Responsibility, Buck Hill Falls, PA. Pittsburgh, PA: Carnegie Press.

Merseth, K. (1991a). *The case for cases in teacher education.* Washington, DC: American Association of Higher Education and the American Association of Colleges for Teacher Education.

Merseth, K. (1991b). The early history of case-based instruction: Insights for teacher education today. *Journal of Teacher Education, 42,* 243–249.

Miller, J. C. (1977). *The wolf by the ears: Thomas Jefferson and slavery.* New York: New American Library.

Nader, R. (1978). Introduction. In J. Seligman, *The high citadel* (pp. xiii–xxv). Boston: Houghton Mifflin.

Nisbett, R. E., & Ross, L. (1980). *Human inference: Strategies and shortcomings of social judgment.* Englewood Cliffs, NJ: Prentice Hall.

Noddings, N. (1984). *Caring: A feminine approach to ethics and moral education.* Los Angeles: University of California Press.

Oakes, J. (1985). *Keeping track.* New Haven, CT: Yale University Press.

Olson, J. (1988). Making sense of teaching: Cognition vs. culture. *Journal of Curriculum Studies, 20,* 167–169.

Osler, W. (1901). Books and men, remarks. *Boston Medical and Surgical Journal, 144,* 60–61.

Osler, W. (1969). On the need of a radical reform in our methods of teaching senior students. In J. P. McGovern & C. G. Roland (Eds.), *William Osler: The continuing education* (pp. 177–192). Springfield, IL: Charles C. Thomas. (Reprinted from *Medical News,* 1903, *82,* 49–53)

Pennoyer, A. (1928). The student-teacher's case-study problems at the Montclair teachers college. *Problems in teacher training* (pp. 289–292). Yonkers-on-Hudson, NY: World Book.

Perry, G., & Perry, P. (1969). *Case studies in teaching.* London: Pittman.

Perry, W. G., Jr. (1970). *Forms of intellectual and ethical development in the college years.* New York: Holt, Rinehart & Winston.

Peters, R. S. (1967). *Ethics and education.* Glenview, IL: Scott, Foresman.

Peters, R. S. (1977). *Education and the education of teachers.* Boston: Routledge & Kegan Paul.

Raths, J. (1971). Worthwhile activities. In J. Raths, J. R. Pancella, & J. S. Van Ness (Eds.), *Studying teaching* (2nd ed) (pp. 131–137). Englewood Cliffs, NJ: Prentice Hall.

Raths, J. (1982). The evaluation of teachers. In Harold I. Mitzel, (Ed.), *Encyclopedia of Educational Research* (Vol. 2; pp. 611–617) (5th ed.). New York: Free Press.

Raths, J., Katz, L., & McAninch, A. (1989). A plight of teacher educators: Clinical mentalities in a scientific culture. In E. Wiesnewski & E. R. Ducharme (Eds.), *The professors of teaching: An inquiry* (pp. 105–118). New York: State University of New York Press.

Raths, L. E., Harmin, M., & Simon, S. B. (1978). *Values and teaching* (2nd ed.). Columbus, OH: Charles E. Merrill.

Redlich, J. (1914). *The common law and the case method in American university law schools.* (Carnegie Foundation Bulletin No. 8). New York: Carnegie Foundation for the Advancement of Teaching.

Reed, A. Z. (1921). *Training for the public profession of the law.* (Carnegie Foundation Bulletin No. 15). New York: Carnegie Foundation for the Advancement of Teaching.

Rosenholtz, S. J. (1985). Effective schools: Interpreting the evidence. *American Journal of Education, 94,* 352–388.

Rosenholtz, S. J. (1989). *Teachers' workplace.* New York: Longman.

Rothstein, W. G. (1987). *American medical schools and the practice of medicine: A history.* New York: Oxford University Press.

Ryan, K. (1980). Biting the apple: An introduction. In K. Ryan, K. K. Newman, G. Mager, J. Applegate, T. Lasley, R. Flora, & J. Johnston, *Biting the apple: Accounts of first year teachers* (pp. 1–19). New York: Longman.

Sanders, D. P., & McCutcheon, G. (1986). The development of practical theories of teaching. *Journal of Curriculum and Supervision, 2,* 50–67.

Schnelle, K. E. (1967). *Case analysis and business problem solving.* New York: McGraw-Hill.

Schofield, J. R. (1984). *New and expanded medical schools, mid-century to the 1980s.* San Francisco: Jossey-Bass.

Schwab, J. (1978a). The practical: A language for curriculum. In I. Westbury & N. J. Wilkof (Eds.), *Science, curriculum and liberal education* (pp. 287–321). Chicago: University of Chicago Press.

Schwab, J. (1978b). The practical: Arts of eclectic. In I. Westbury & N. J. Wilkof (Eds.), *Science, curriculum and liberal education* (pp. 322–364). Chicago: University of Chicago Press.

Scriven, M. (1979). Clinical judgment. In H. T. Engelhardt Jr., S. F. Spiker, & B. Towers (Eds.), *Clinical judgment: A critical appraisal* (pp. 3–16). Dordrect, Holland: D. Reidel.

Scully, M. (1983, May 4). Harvard's Bok urges changing 'expensive, inefficient' legal system. *Chronicle of Higher Education,* p. 8.

Sergiovanni, T. J. (1985). Landscapes, mindscapes and reflective practice in supervision. *Journal of Curriculum and Supervision, 1,* 5–17.

Shermis, S. S. (1967). *Philosophic foundations of education.* New York: American Book Company.

Shulman, J. H., Colbert, J. A., Kemper, D., & Dmytriw, L. (1990). Case writing as a site for collaboration. *Teacher Education Quarterly, 17,* 63–78.

Shulman, L. S. (1984). The practical and the eclectic: A deliberation on teaching and educational research. *Curriculum Inquiry, 14,* 183–200.

Shulman, L. S. (1986). Those who understand: Knowledge growth in teaching. *Educational Researcher, 15,* 4–14.

Shulman, L. S. (1987). The wisdom of practice: Managing complexity in medicine and teaching. In D. C. Berliner & B. V. Rosenshine (Eds.), *Talks to teachers: A Festschrift for N. L. Gage.* (pp. 369–386). New York: Random House.

Shulman, L. S. (1992). Toward a pedagogy of cases. In J. Shulman (Ed.), *Case methods in teacher education* (pp. 1–30). New York: Teachers College Press.

Shuman, R. B. (1989). *Classroom encounters: Problems, case studies, solutions.* Washington, DC: National Education Association.

Slavin, R. E. (1983). *Cooperative learning.* New York: Longman.

Smith, G. (1987). The use and effectiveness of the case study method in management education: A critical review. *Management Education and Development, 18*, 51–61.

Smith, L. M., & Geoffrey, W. (1968). *The complexities of an urban classroom.* New York: Holt, Rinehart & Winston.

Sperle, D. H. (1933). *The case method technique in professional training.* New York: Teachers College, Columbia University.

Starr, P. (1982). *The social transformation of American medicine.* New York: Basic Books.

Stevens, R. (1970). Aging mistress: The law school in America. *Change in Higher Education, 2*, 32–42.

Stevens, R. (1983). *Law school.* Chapel Hill, NC: University of North Carolina Press.

Stone, L. (1987). Book review of Belenky, et al., *Women's Ways of Knowing. Teachers College Record, 89*, 307–312.

Sykes, G. (1989). Learning to teach with cases. *Colloquy, 2*, 7–13. East Lansing, MI: National Center for Research on Teaching, Michigan State University.

Sykes, G., & Bird, T. (1992). Teacher education and the case idea. In G. Grant (Ed.), *Review of Research in Education* (Vol. 18, pp. 457–521). Washington, DC: American Educational Research Association.

Teich, P. (1986). Research on American law teaching: Is there a case against the case system? *Journal of Legal Education, 36*, 167–188.

Teaching with cases at the Harvard Business School. (1987). In C. R. Christensen (Ed.), *Teaching and the case method* (pp. 16–49). Boston: Harvard Business School.

Thies-Sprinthall, L., & Sprinthall, N. A. (1987). Preservice teachers as adult learners: A new framework for teacher education. In M. Haberman & J. M. Backus (Eds.), *Advances in teacher education* (Vol. 3, pp. 35–56). Norwood, NJ: Ablex.

Thorne, B. (1973). Professional education in medicine. In E. C. Hughes, B. Thorne, A. M. DeBaggis, A. Gurin, and D. Williams (Eds.), *Education for the professions of medicine, law, theology, and social welfare* (pp. 17–98). New York: McGraw-Hill.

Tom, A. R. (1984). *Teaching as a moral craft.* New York: Longman.

Towl, A. R. (1969). *To study administration by cases.* Boston: Harvard University Graduate School of Business Administration.

Towle, C. (1954). *The learner in education for the professions.* Chicago: University of Chicago Press.

Walberg, H. J. (1986). Syntheses of research on teaching. In M. C. Wittrock (Ed.), *Handbook of research on teaching* (3rd ed., pp. 214–229). New York: Macmillan.

Waller, W. (1967). *The sociology of teaching.* New York: John Wiley & Sons. (Original work published 1932.)

Waples, D. (1927). *Problems in classroom method.* New York: Macmillan.

Westbury, I. (1973). Conventional classrooms, "open" classrooms, and the technology of teaching. *Journal of Curriculum Studies, 5*, 99–121.

Westbury, I., & Wilkof, N. J. (1978). Introduction. In I. Westbury & N. J. Wilkof (Eds.), *Science, curriculum, and liberal education* (pp. 1–40). Chicago: University of Chicago Press.

Wiebe, R. H. (1984). *The opening of American society.* New York: Alfred A. Knopf.

Yinger, R. J. (1987). Learning the language of practice. *Curriculum Inquiry, 17,* 293–317.

Zeichner, K., & Tabachnick, B. R. (1981). Are the effects of university teacher education 'washed out' by school experience? *Journal of Teacher Education, 32,* 7–11.

INDEX

About the Author

Amy Raths McAninch graduated in 1978 from Kirkland College in Clinton, New York, with a B.A. in economics. She worked as a research assistant for the Brookings Institution before beginning graduate work in the department of educational policy studies in the College of Education at the University of Illinois. She received her M.S. in 1985 and her Ph.D. with a concentration in philosophy of education in 1989. She has taught at Washington University and Knox College in Galesburg, Illinois, and is currently an assistant professor in the department of education of St. Mary College, Leavenworth, Kansas.